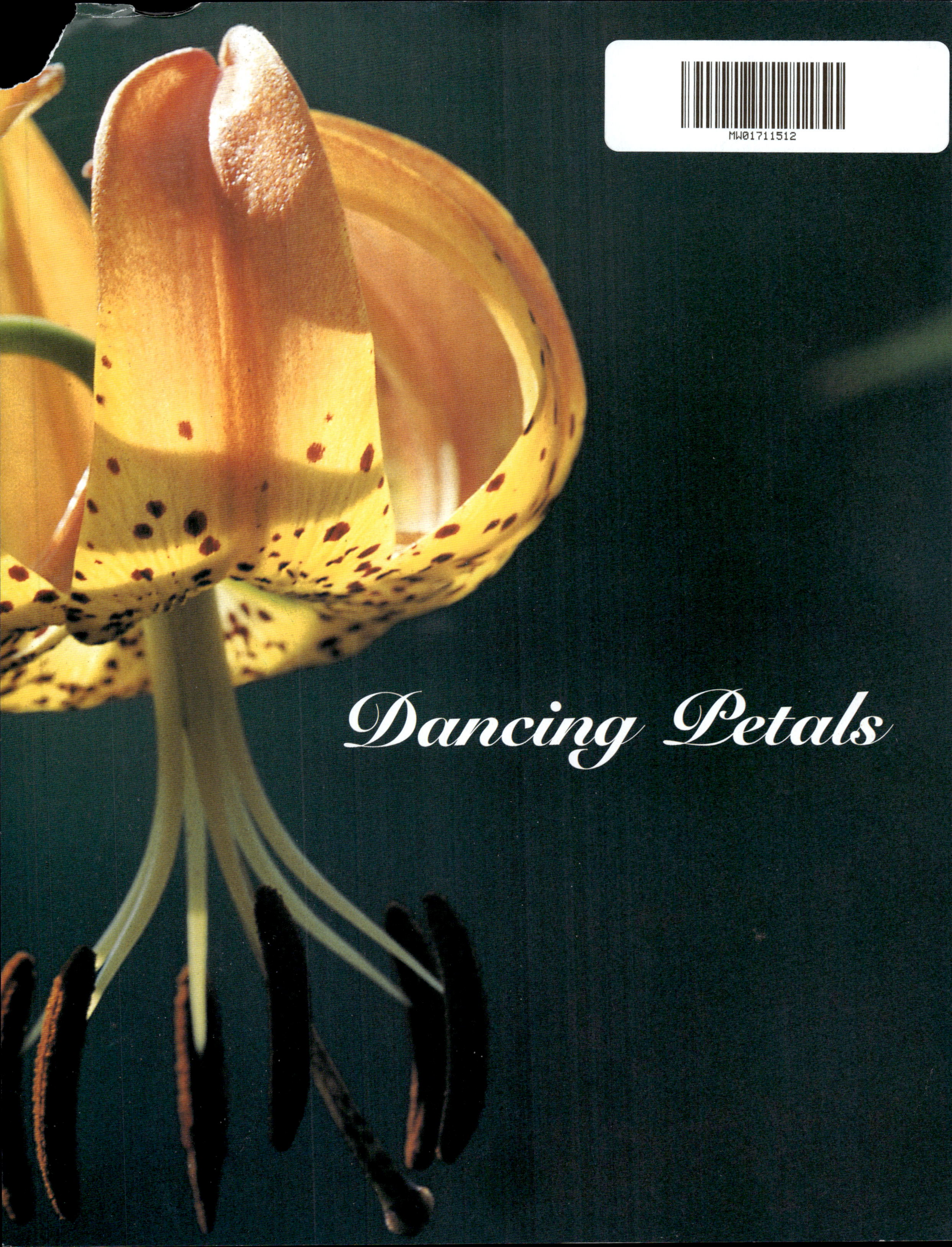

Dancing Petals

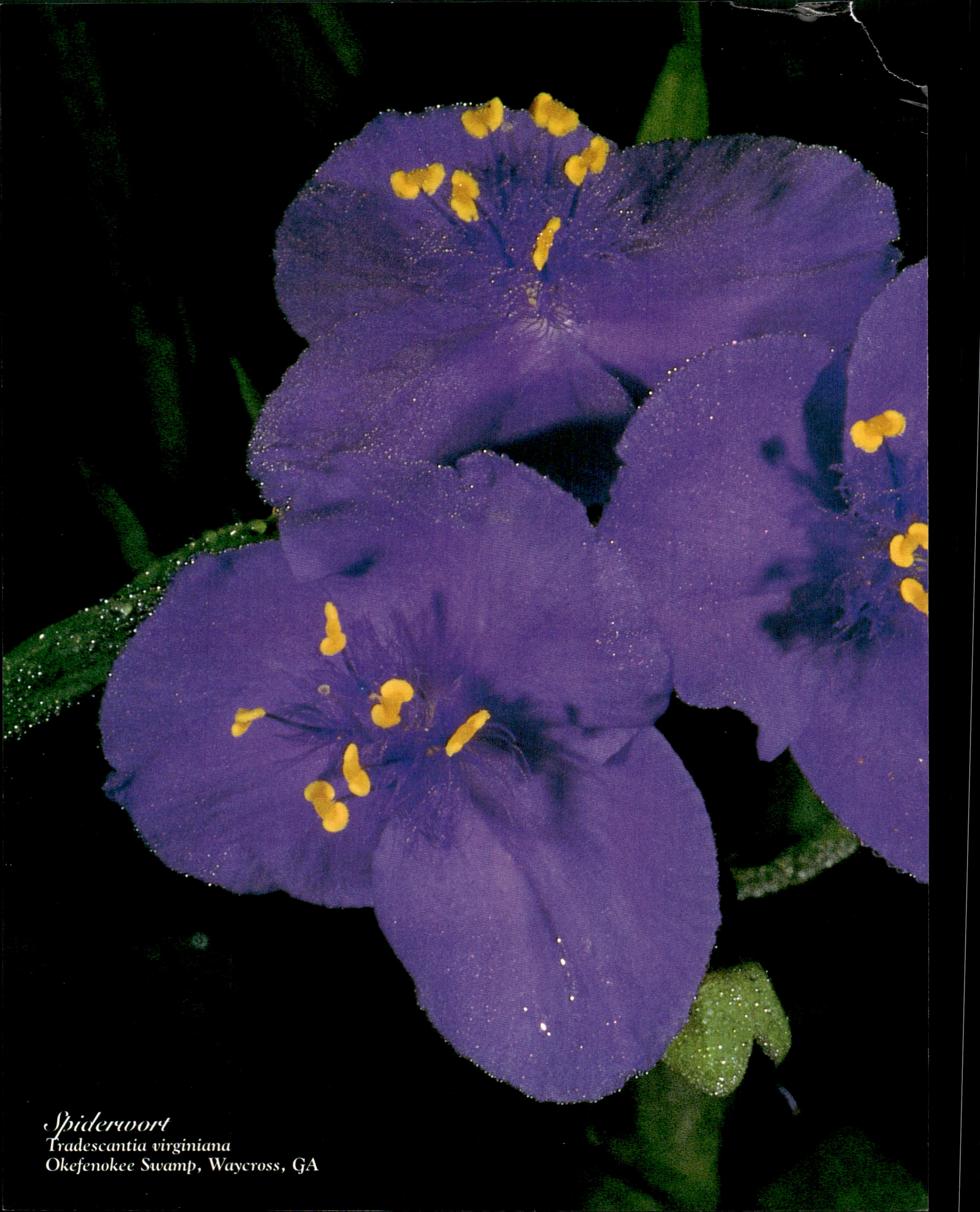

Spiderwort
Tradescantia virginiana
Okefenokee Swamp, Waycross, GA

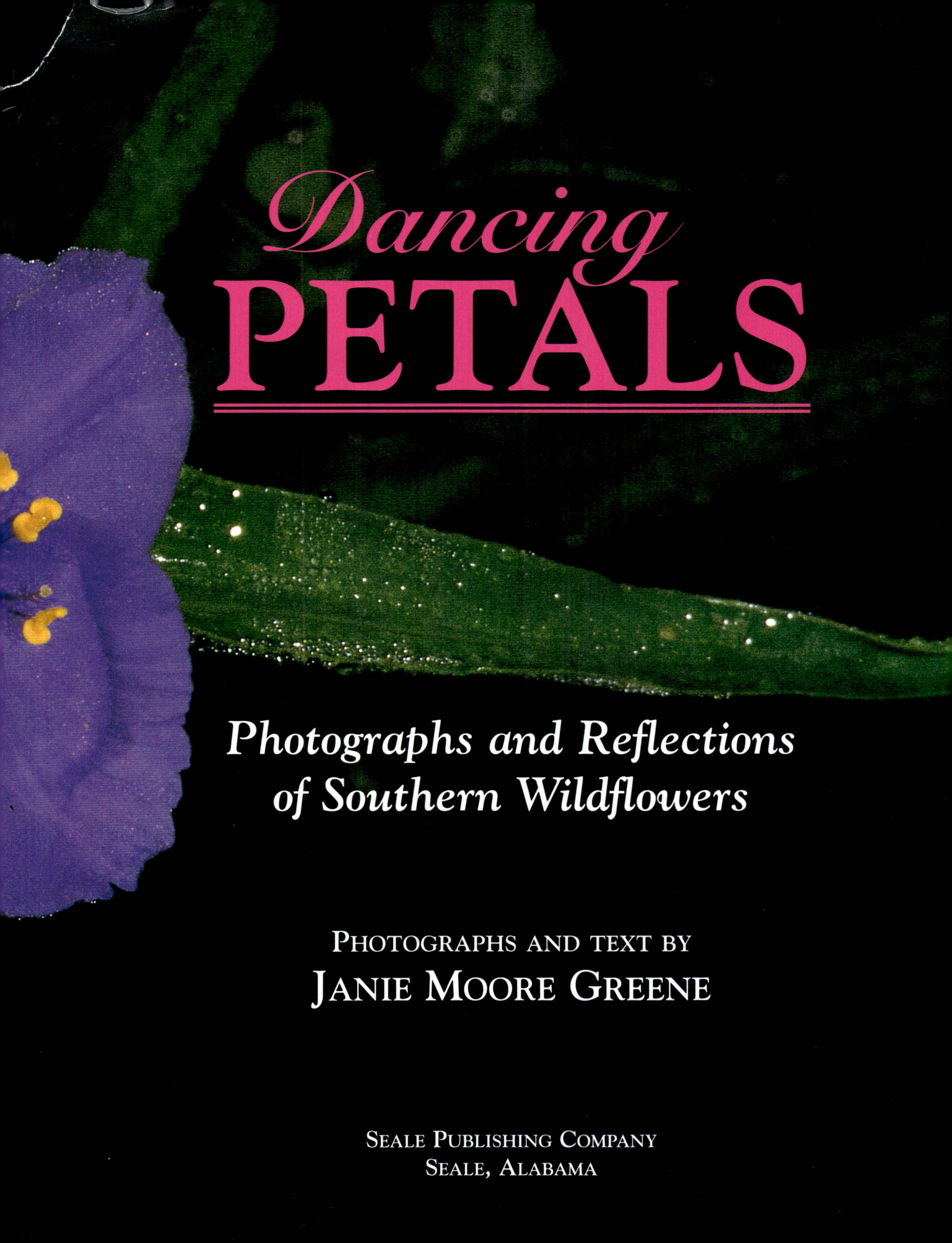

Dancing PETALS

Photographs and Reflections of Southern Wildflowers

PHOTOGRAPHS AND TEXT BY
JANIE MOORE GREENE

SEALE PUBLISHING COMPANY
SEALE, ALABAMA

Library of Congress Cataloging-in-Publication Data

Greene, Janie M., 1998
Dancing Feathers / Janie Moore Greene - First Edition
Bibliography

Text edited by Linda Tomblin

Design Consultant, Ed Symmes

Computer layout, Connie Romanishan

Equipment used to design this book: Minolta & Canon 35 mm Cameras, Power MacIntosh using Adobe Photoshop and Quark Xpress.

This 1998 edition published and produced by

SAN 298-2714

Seale Publishing Company
P.O. Box 65
Seale, AL 36875
Tel: 334-855-2772 or 800-725-4619
Fax 334-855-2767

First Edition 1998

ISBN 0-9641570-2-0 (soft copy)

ISBN 0-9641570-3-9 (hard copy)

Library of Congress Catalog Number 94-92095

Printed in Singapore

Front cover photo: Pink Lady's-slipper, Moccasin flower, Cypripedium acaule
Photographed in Botanical Gardens: Highlands, NC
Back cover photo: Atamasco Lily, Zephyranthes atamasco
Photographed on Hwy 19-98, south of Perry, FL

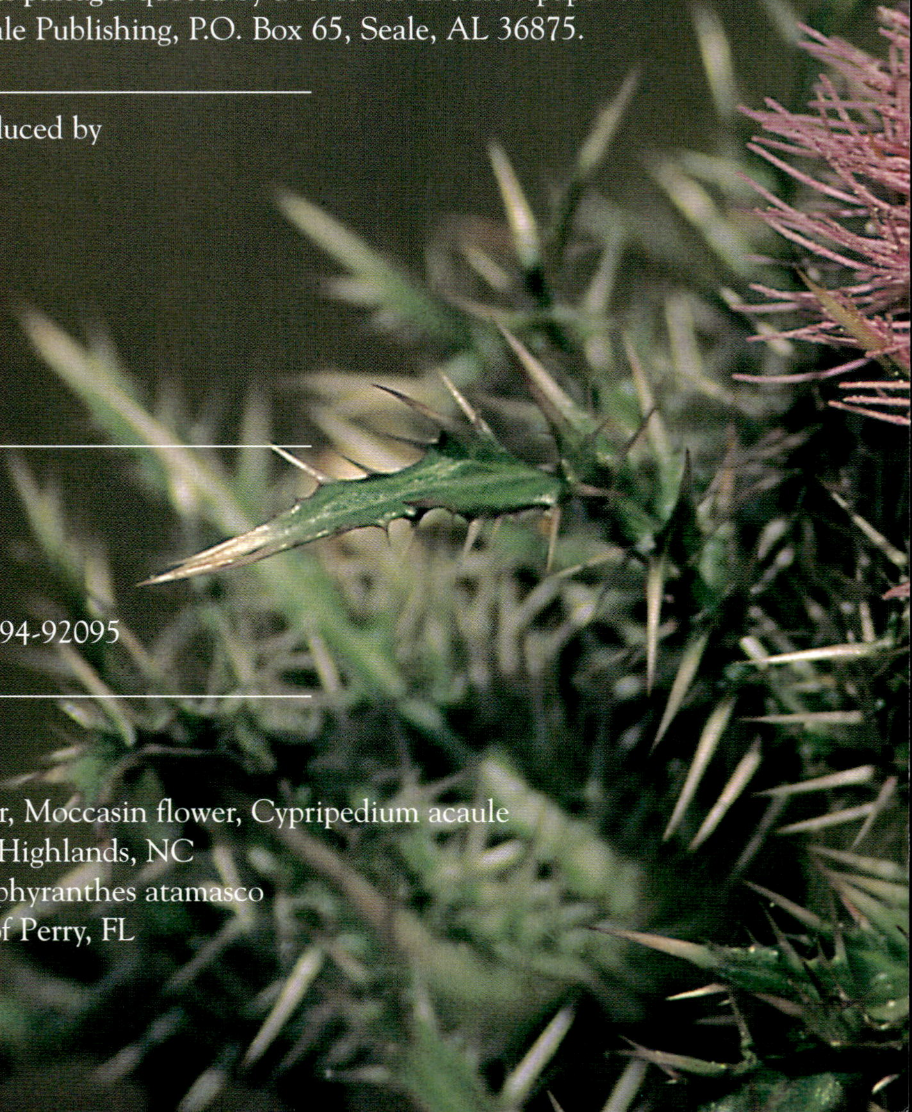

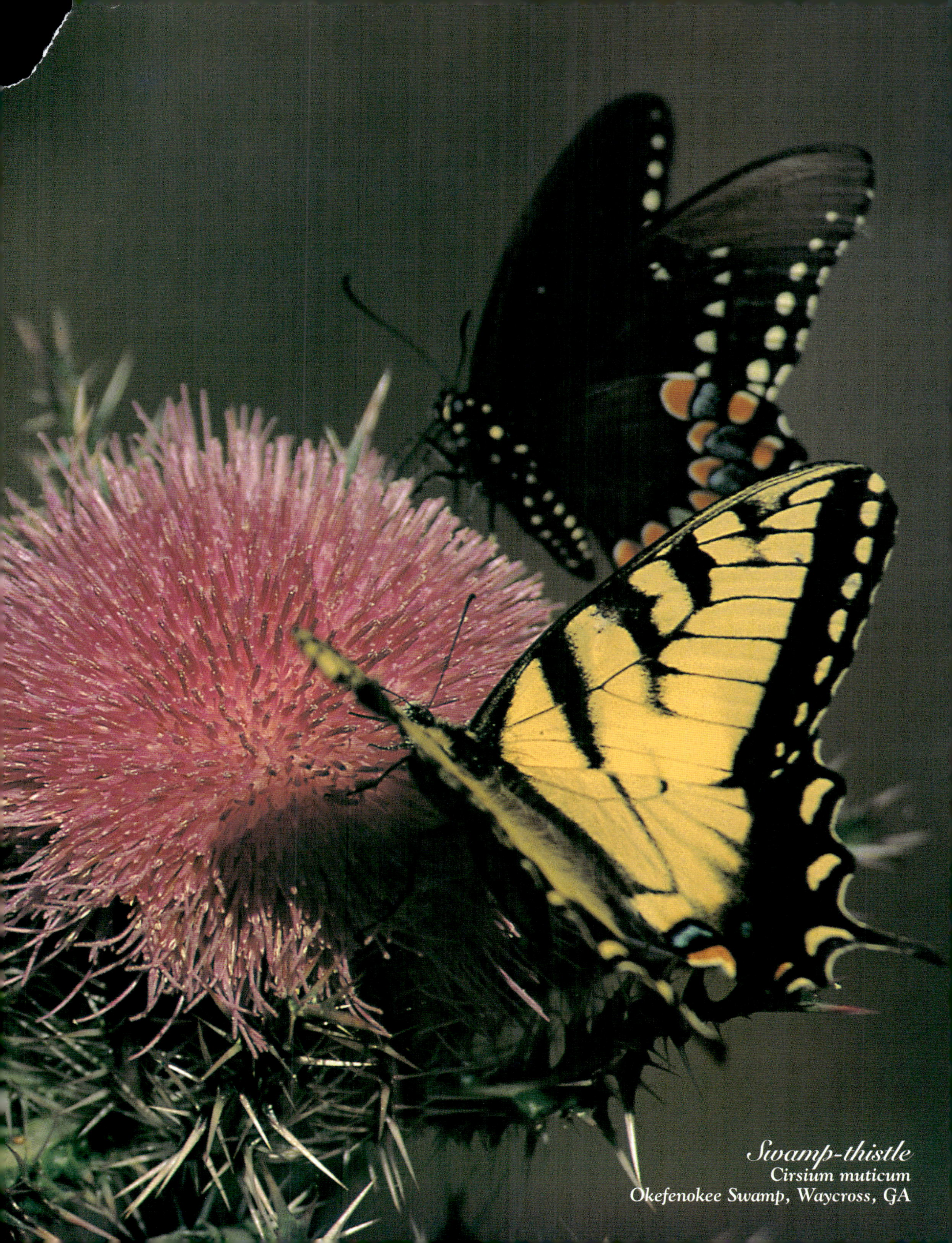

Swamp-thistle
Cirsium muticum
Okefenokee Swamp, Waycross, GA

Acknowledgements

I would like to express sincere appreciation and a heartfelt thanks to those who helped me compile DANCING PETALS:

Linda Tomblin, my collaborator and friend of many years, for her dedicated encouragement, time, and energy to this book project;

Connie Romanishan, computer layout;

Ed Symmes, consultant and designer;

Dorothy Gibson, typesetter and computer assistant;

Betty Persons, my valuable photography assistant;

Dr. Marion Motley Carchache for her expert text advice;

Dr. Gilbert Ramsey, Angela Burns, Judy Jackson, Jane Pidcock & Virginia Quillian, for their manuscript critiques;

Ron Enfinger for laboriously scanning the photographs;

Claudine Laabs, my photography buddy;

Dennis Paramore, D.O.T. in Dawson GA for his help in identifying wildflowers;

Bill Wykle many thanks for his help in identifying and finding wildflowers;

The Florida Publishers Association, especially Betsy Lampe & Chris Carroll;

Lorraine Tufts, for her publishing advice.

Always my appreciation goes to my husband, friend, camera-bearer, financier, and love of forty-five years, Roy Greene, and the rest of my beautiful family: Mama, Lynne, Keith, Katie, Leslie Anne, Susan, Mitch, Sandy, Roy III, Janie Lynne, Ashley, Dan, Leslie, John Daniel, Dudley, David, Rosanna, Muriel, Leslie, and Juan.

Last of all, to my Heavenly Father who gave me His divine inspiration, guidance and grace to complete the work involved in this book project.

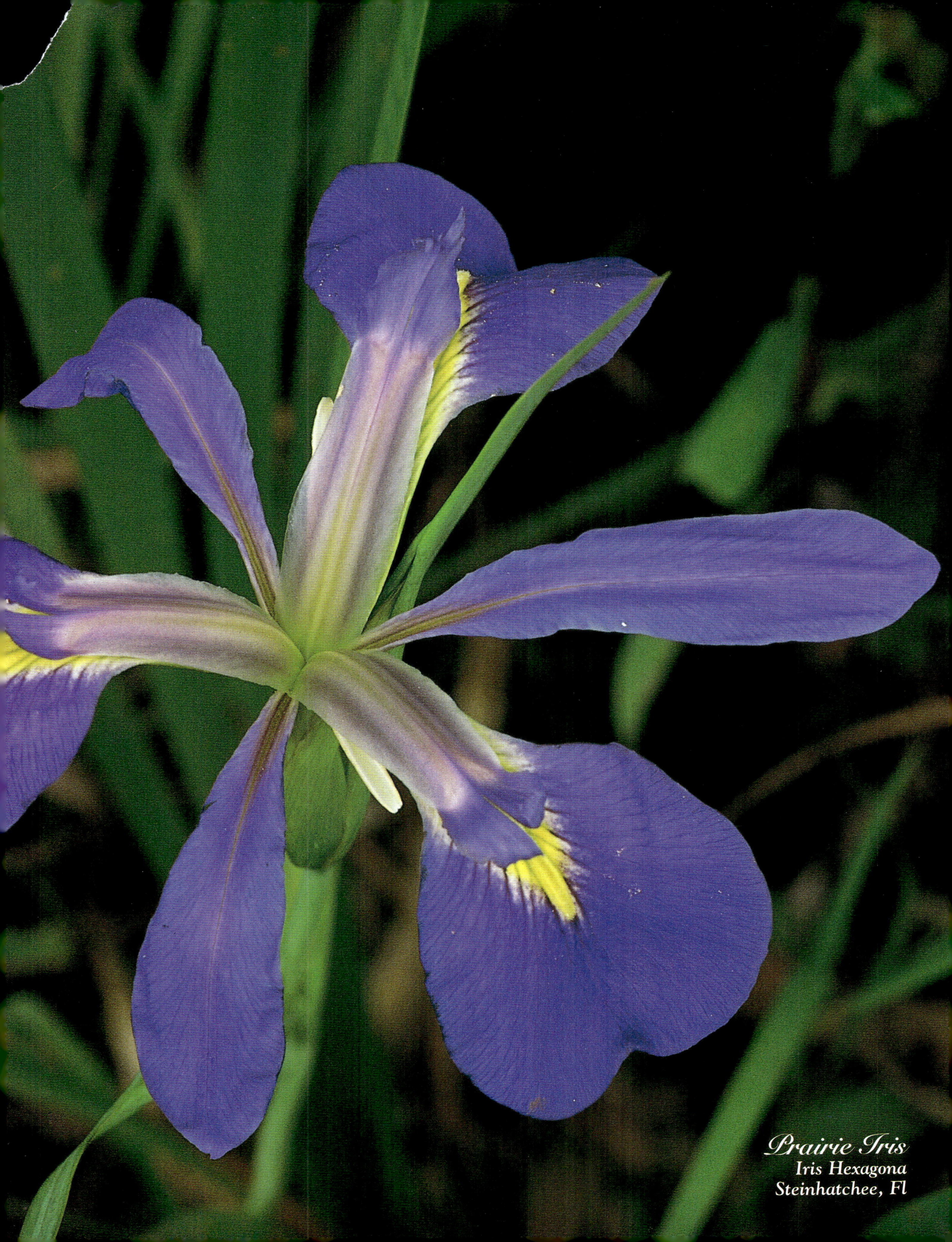

Prairie Iris
Iris Hexagona
Steinhatchee, Fl

Dedication

To my mother, Loretta Moore, who gave me the gift of a seed planted in my memory of her love of wildflowers.

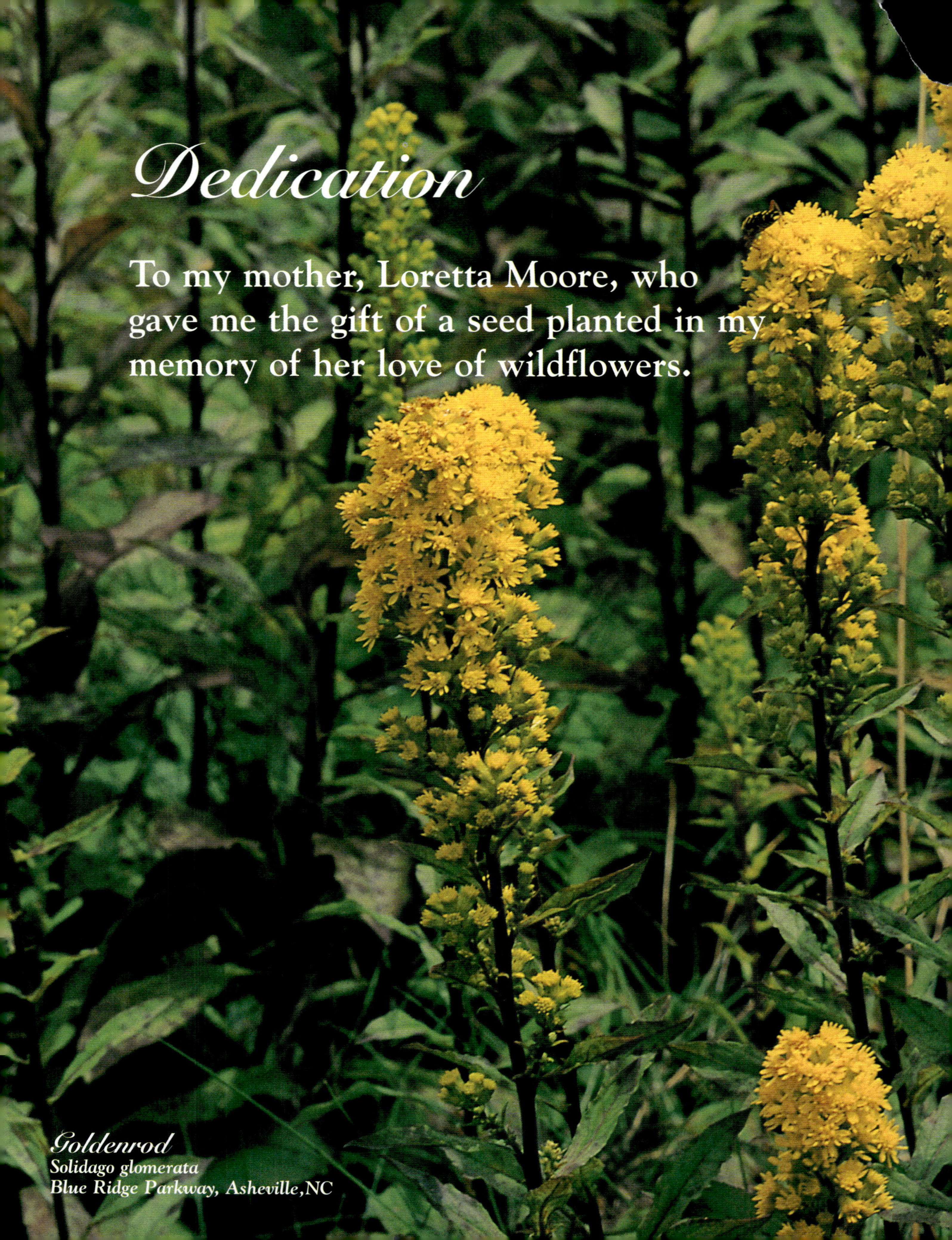

Goldenrod
Solidago glomerata
Blue Ridge Parkway, Asheville,NC

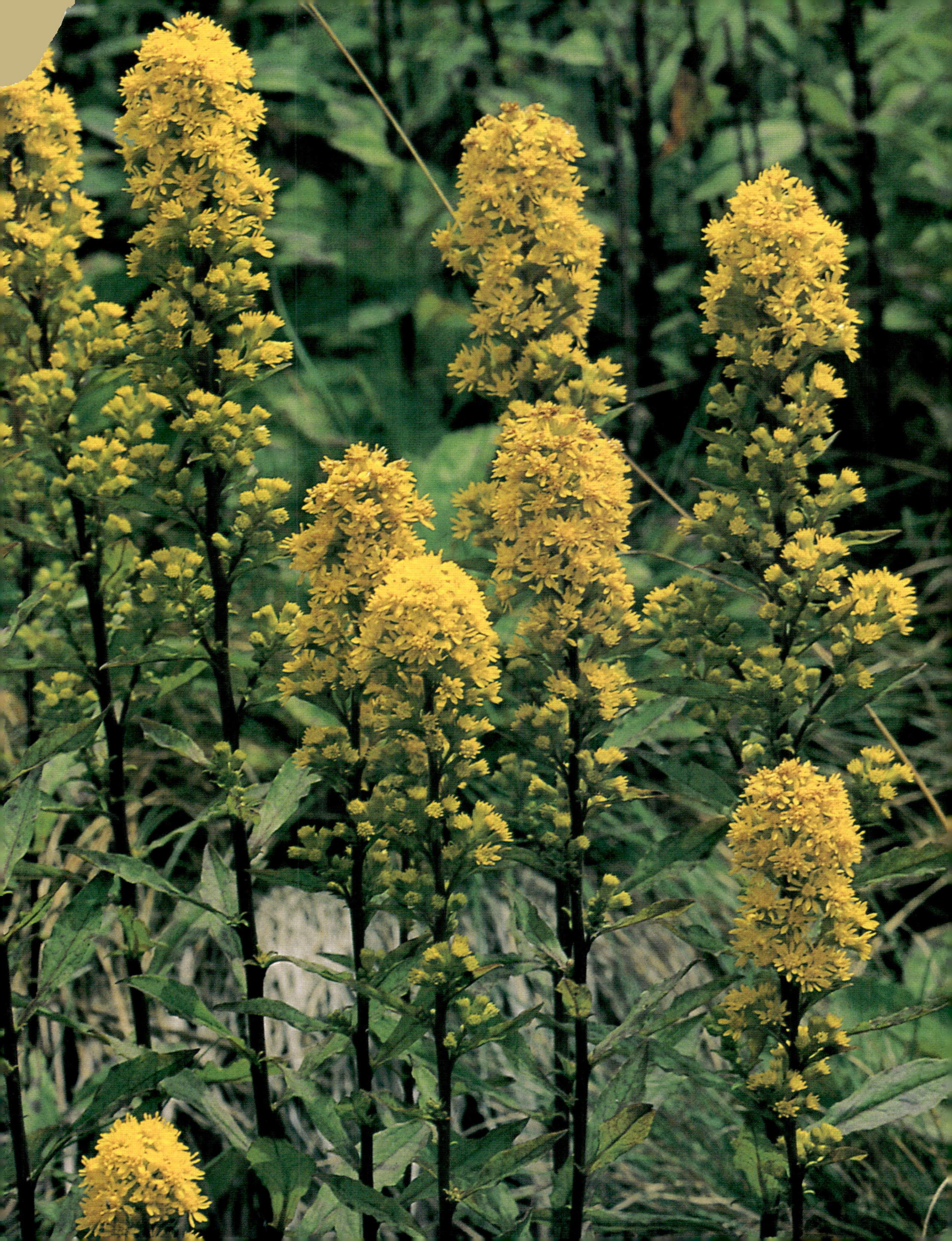

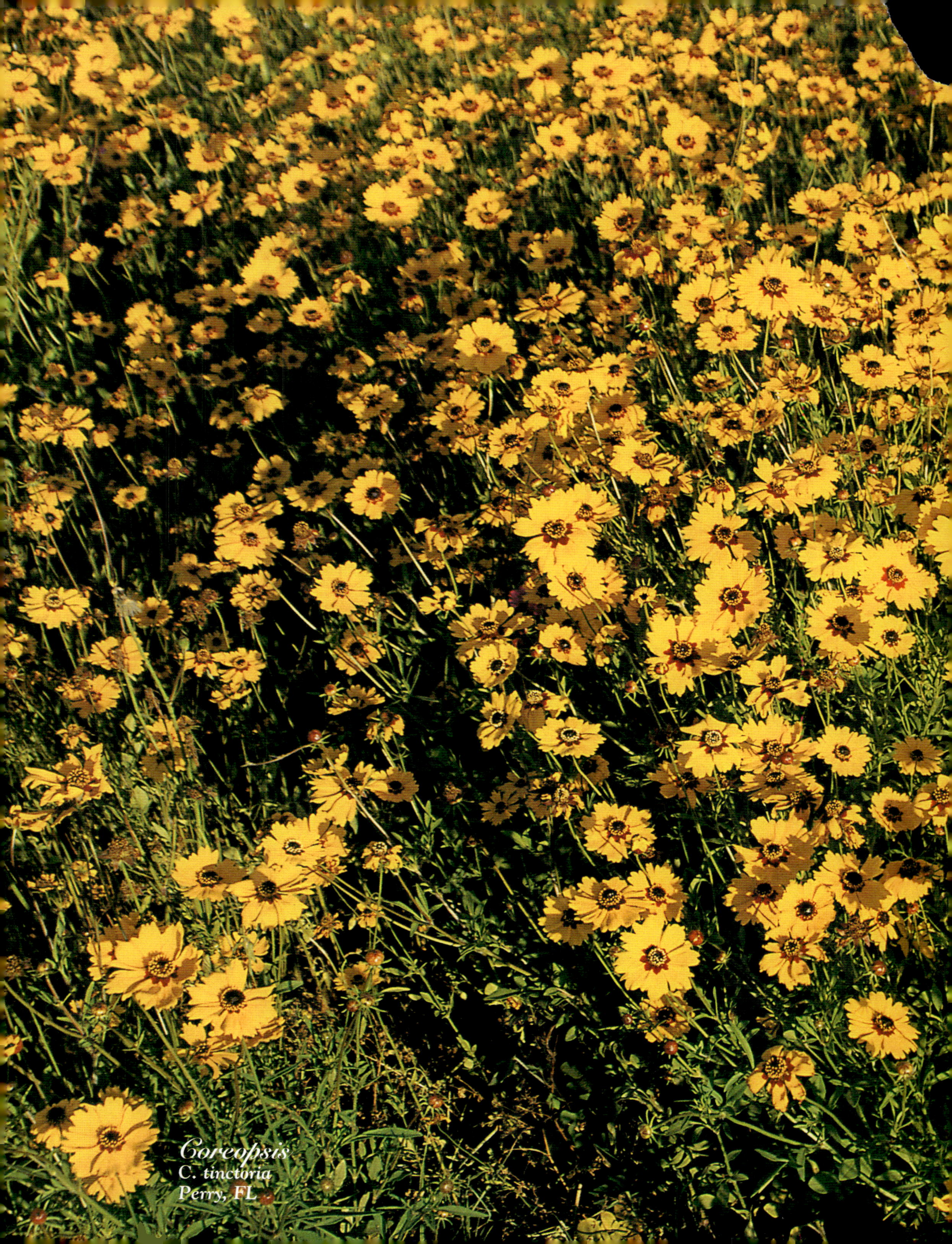

Coreopsis
C. tinctoria
Perry, FL

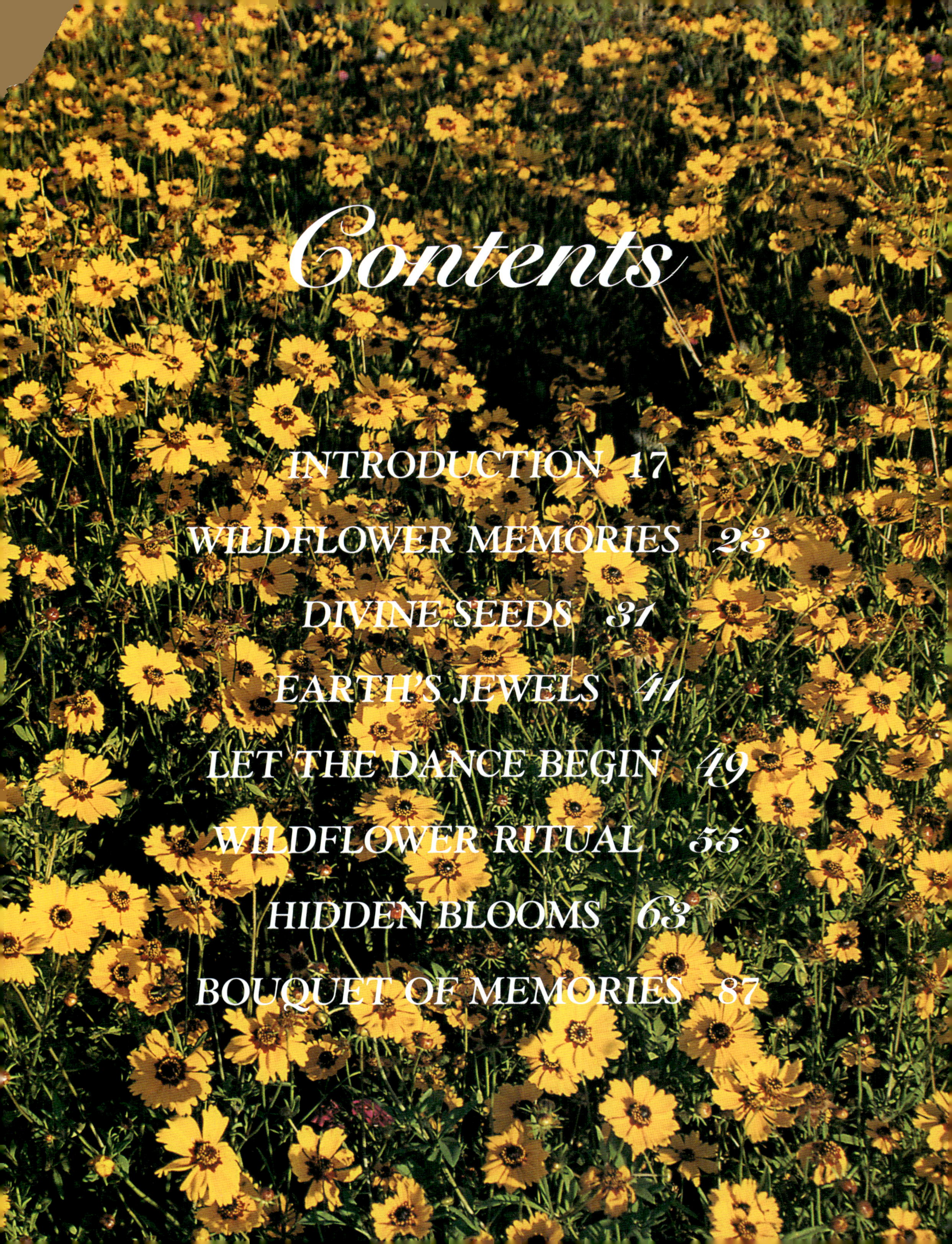

Contents

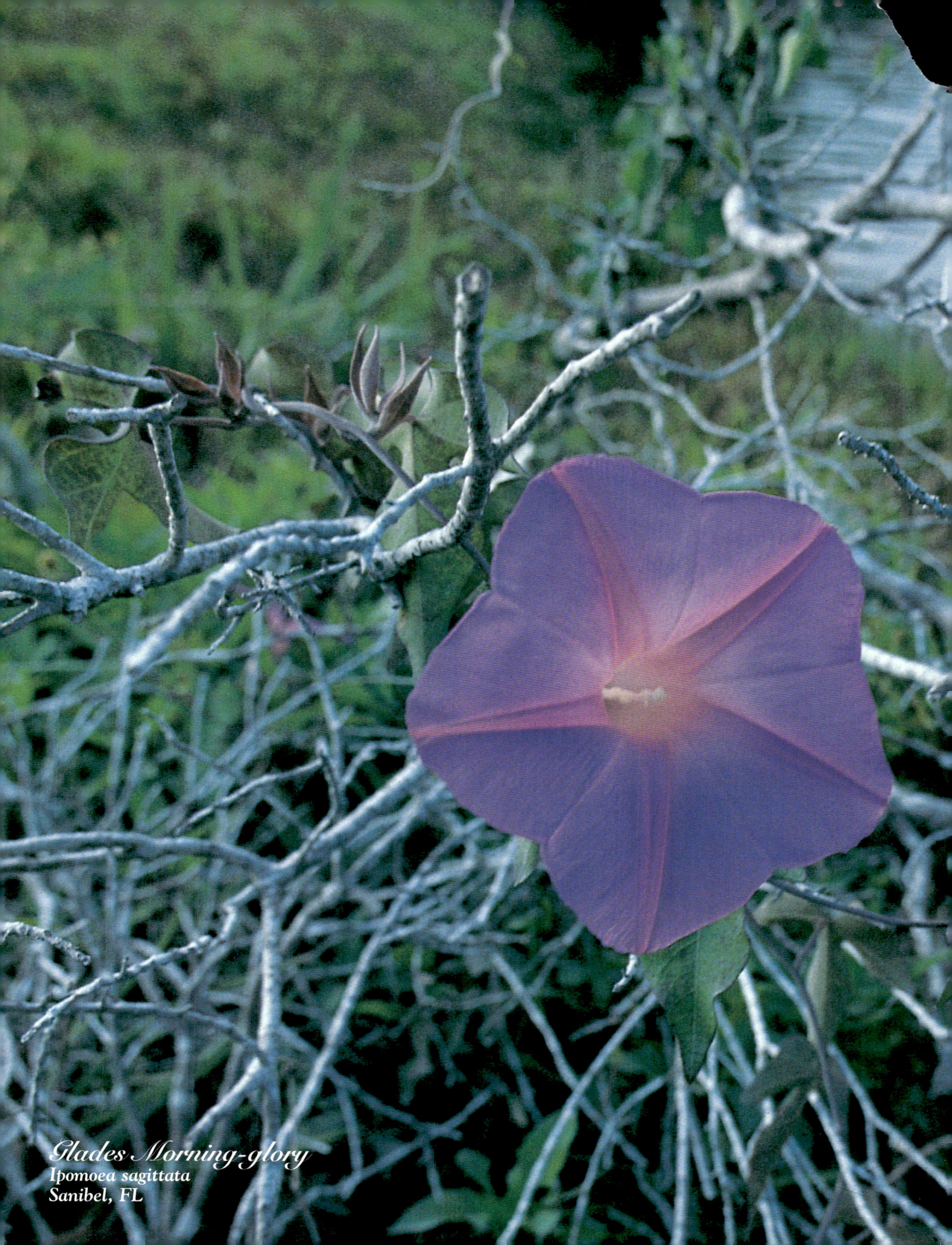

Glades Morning-glory
Ipomoea sagittata
Sanibel, FL

Introduction

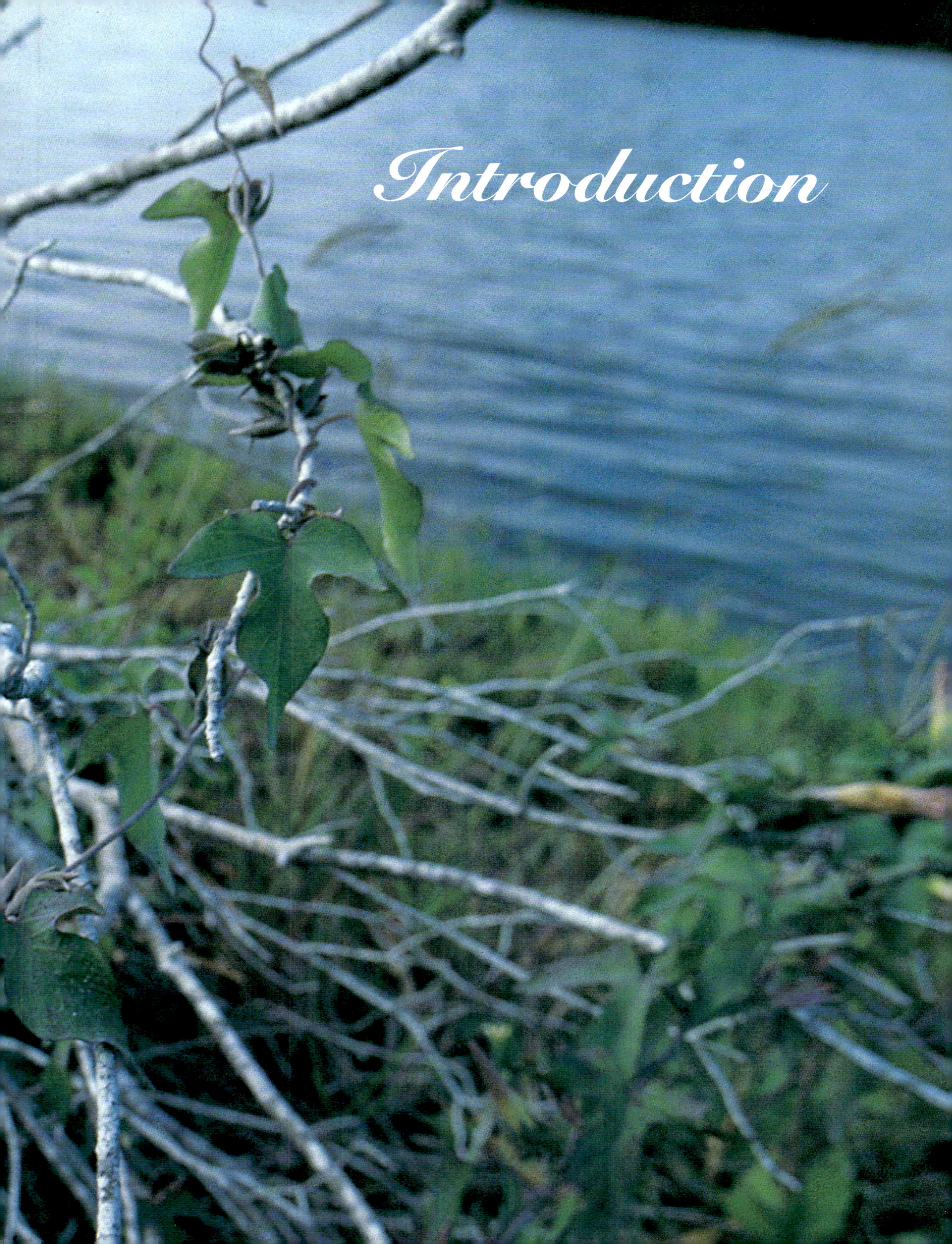

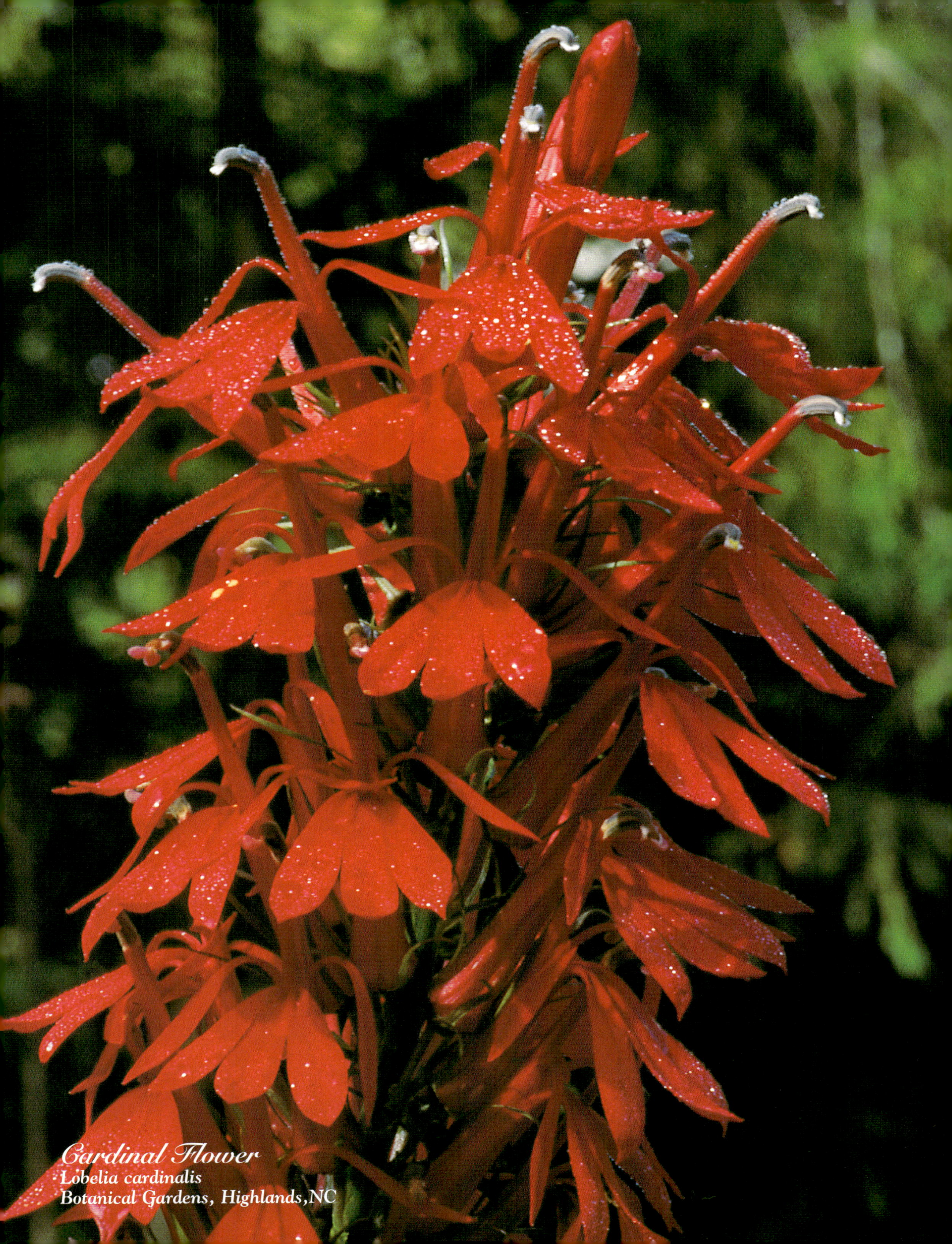

Cardinal Flower
Lobelia cardinalis
Botanical Gardens, Highlands, NC

Introduction

"I was raised by the song of the murmuring grove
and loving I learned among flowers."
Fredrick Holderlin (Tr.T.Cole)

Since I'm a Southerner and thoroughly grounded in the South, I wanted this wildflower book to be born from my own groundedness....my roots. I've always loved telling stories and listening to the stories of others. Therefore, the reflections in *Dancing Petals* are short stories taken from my life and used as a vehicle through which I've woven a thread of an inspirational theme. I've included memories and narratives from my childhood, my marriage, and my family, and have interlaced some of life's simple but valuable lessons through these experiences. I also love to photograph nature, so I combined my love of storytelling and my love of nature photography to create *Dancing Petals*. The pictures in this book are from several wildflower photographic expeditions I made in Florida, Georgia, Alabama, and North Carolina. There are photographs of a Colombine, a Pink and a Yellow Lady's slipper, Easter Lilies, Carolina Lilies, Dwarf Crested Irises, Violets and many other kinds of wildflowers indigenous to the Southeastern United States.

Anne Guilfoyle, a former Audubon magazine editor, suggested the title of this book when I asked her advice about the photographs to include in my first book, *Dancing Feathers*. "Leave the wildflowers out," she said. "Use only the wading birds. Then do another book using your wildflowers and call it *Dancing Petals*." With those words, the seeds for *Dancing Petals* were planted inside of me.

Wildflowers are a delight to see, touch, and smell. Soft, velvety, serene, pure in form, colorful and full of truth, they speak to the heart and mind and lift it into a kind of exhilarating joy. They can be seen anywhere...on a hillside, in the meadows, or along the roads. I often see them when my husband, Roy, and I are returning home from one of his fishing trips. Usually we catch a glimpse of them in the spring as we go whizzing by in our comfortable automobiles, hurrying from place to place, but by the time we finally decide to stop, a week or two later, they're almost gone.

We should all take the time to enjoy them along life's way. For as Thoreau said, "Heaven lies at your feet as well as over your head." I believe that Nature is truly humanity's gift from God. And oftentimes, in our hasty living we forget about earth's smaller treasures and their value to our souls. In our hours and days of rushing, we forget that the soul, at times, needs stillness. It should be grounded, and lay fallow as a field of wildflowers must lay fallow before they bloom.

So I invite you to come with me now, to take a little time, to dance with me through the petals. Discover that deep sense of stillness within you when you look into the center of a wildflower. As it speaks to you, let the creativity bubble up out of your soul, like clear springs that stir beneath the ground of your being. Bring your paint brushes, sketch pad, journal, camera or other vehicle of creativity. Use your imagination. Walk your own path through the pages of *Dancing Petals*. Unearth the remarkable and extraordinary jewels of your life,...your unique individuality,...the divine and holy seeds lying dormant within you, your truth.

For the first time in your life, perhaps, give yourself some quiet moments to sit among the seeds of your own sacred ground. Allow the wildflowers of your soul to bloom. Listen to your music, and let the dance begin!

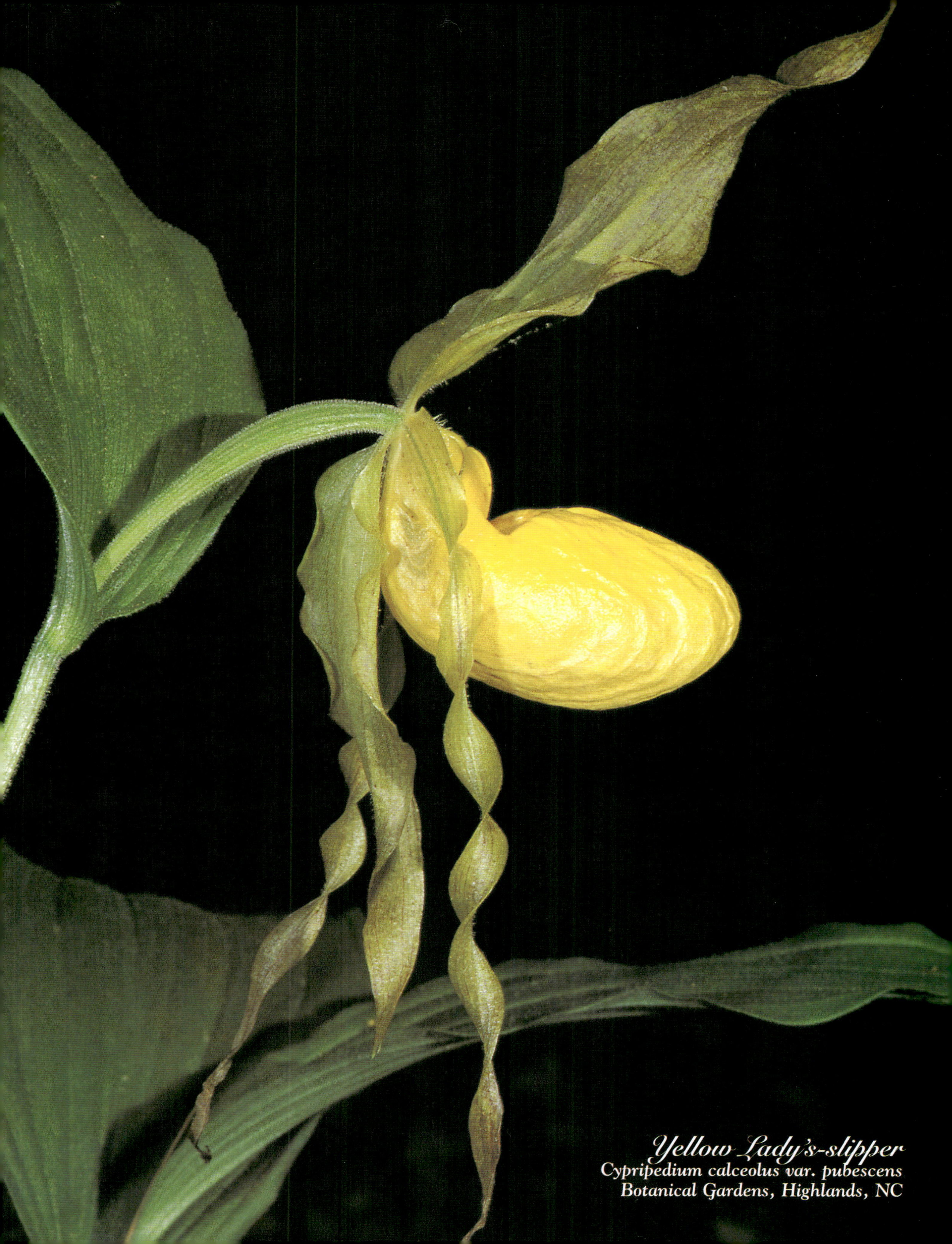

Yellow Lady's-slipper
Cypripedium calceolus var. pubescens
Botanical Gardens, Highlands, NC

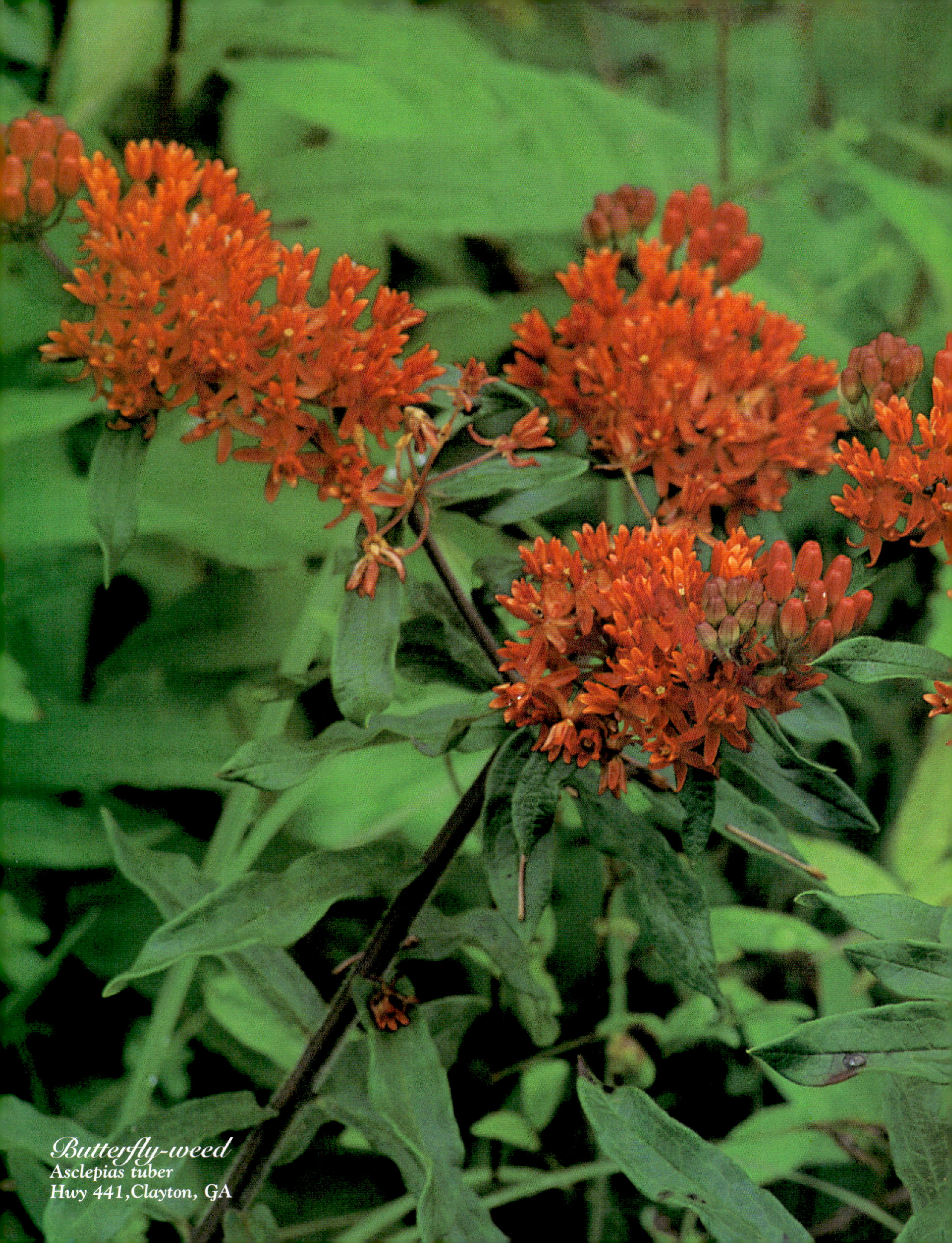
Butterfly-weed
Asclepias tuber
Hwy 441, Clayton, GA

Wildflower Memories

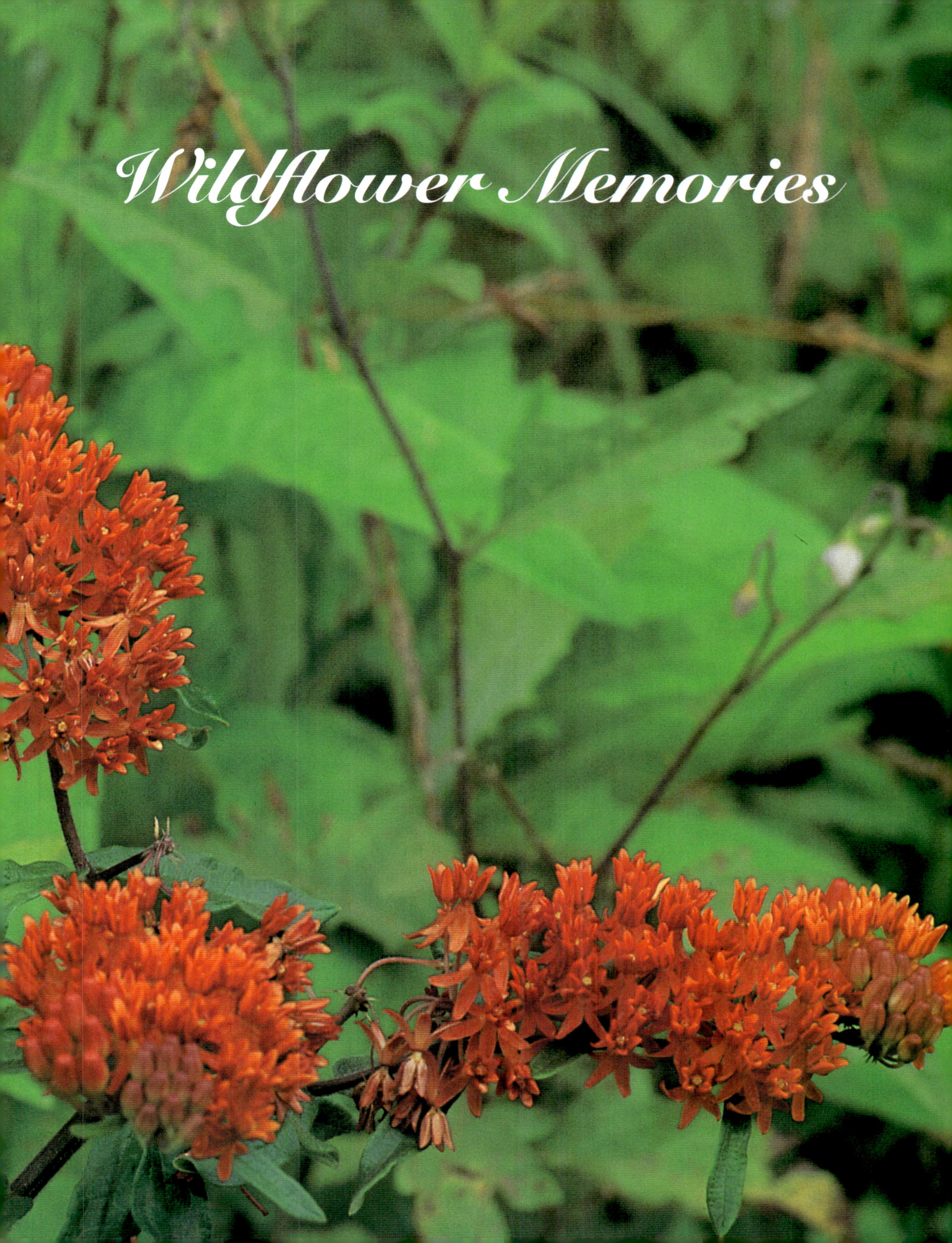

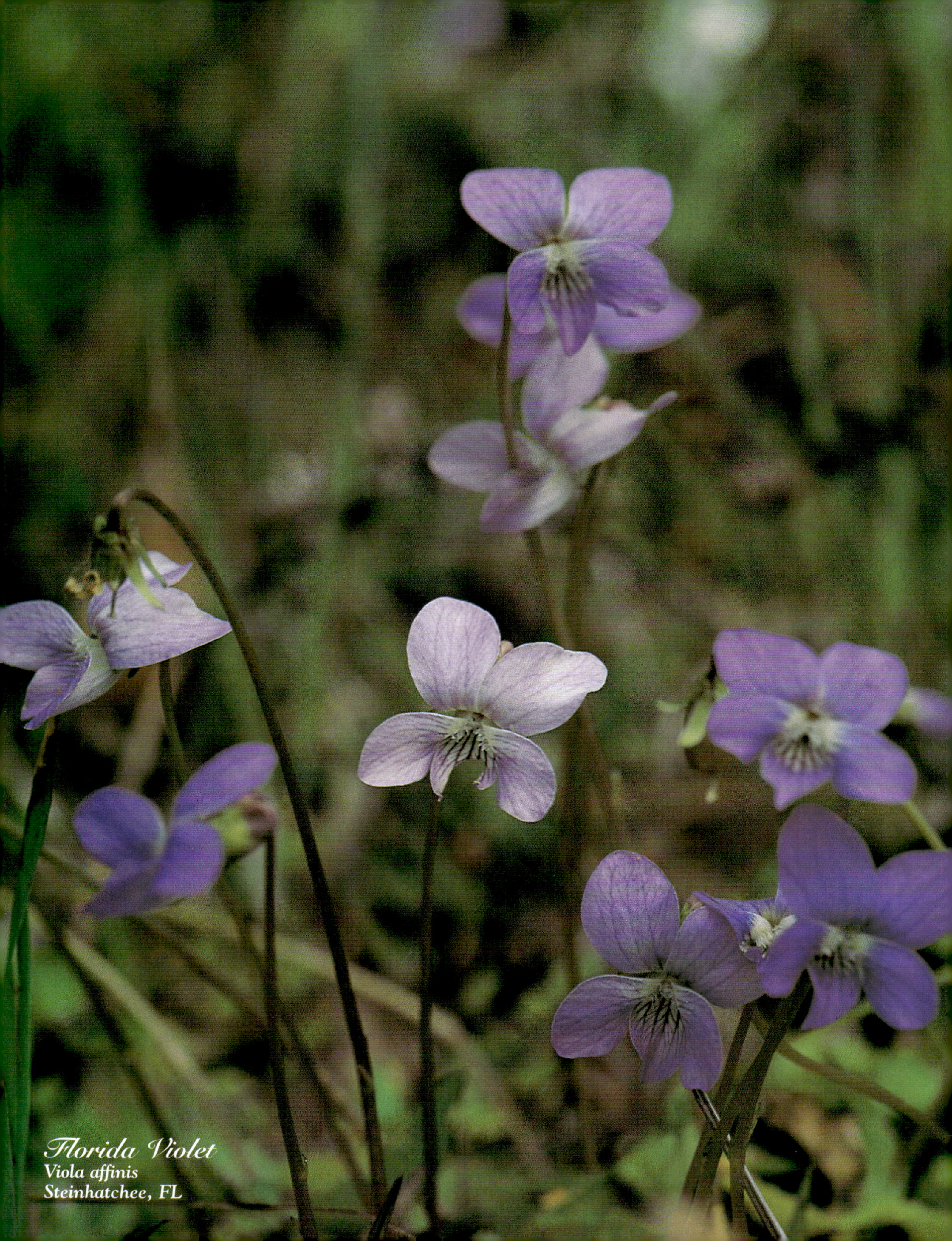

Florida Violet
Viola affinis
Steinhatchee, FL

Wildflower Memories

"Blue! Gentle cousin of the forest-green, married to green in all the sweetest flowers- forget-me-not, the blue bell, and that queen of secrecy, the violet."

John Keats

One spring day recently, I was sitting on half of our luggage in the Atlanta Airport parking lot waiting for my husband, Roy, to come back from the baggage claim with the other half. As I sat watching people rush past, I heard the screams of the huge jet engines over my head and felt the roaring motors vibrate my body as they flew in and out. I looked down at my feet and saw a lilac Confederate Violet struggling to bloom through a crack in the sea of concrete. It reminded me of the violets my friends and I picked at my childhood birthday party in the 1930s...my first wildflower memory. I chuckled to myself as I thought of the extreme contrast between life now at the busy, sophisticated airport and the simple life we lived at the time we celebrated my party in Pineview, Georgia, only 100 miles south.

It was April 5, 1938. The country was in a great depression, but there was nothing depressed about me. It was my sixth birthday. My friends and I gathered in a circle around my mother under the spreading limbs of a hundred-year-old Magnolia tree in our front yard. The leaves shed by the old tree that winter still crackled beneath our energetic feet as though we were stepping on huge piles of newspaper. My pretty, round-faced mother, her long black hair wrapped in a roll around the back of her head in the style of the 1930s, stood in the center of the circle.

"All right, children," she said in her soft southern voice. "I know where we can find lots of violets and Easter Lilies behind the house." We listened as she told us about a damp area along Cobb Creek where wildflowers grew. "If you'll follow me, we'll see who can pick the most wildflowers to take home with you. You might even find some sweet honeysuckle," she said, smiling as she led my friends, James, Sammy, Angela, Helen Bridges, Billy Mann, my brother, David, and me to the creek bank behind our house. Her flared print dress circled around her legs as she walked away. When we saw the scattered white lilies and purple violets, we ran to gather them as though they were Easter eggs. Each one of us tried to collect as many as possible before returning to the house, like Mama did when she was an eleven-year-old. During her lonely hours she'd entertain herself by searching for scattered wildflowers.

She said when she was a little girl her family lived on their old homestead at Cedar Creek near Pineview. When I questioned her about how her wildflower interest developed, she answered, "It was really very beautiful there although I didn't appreciate it too much then. The Cypress trees dripped gray Spanish Moss, so graceful and pretty, I'd press it against my face and feel its softness. I especially liked to see it

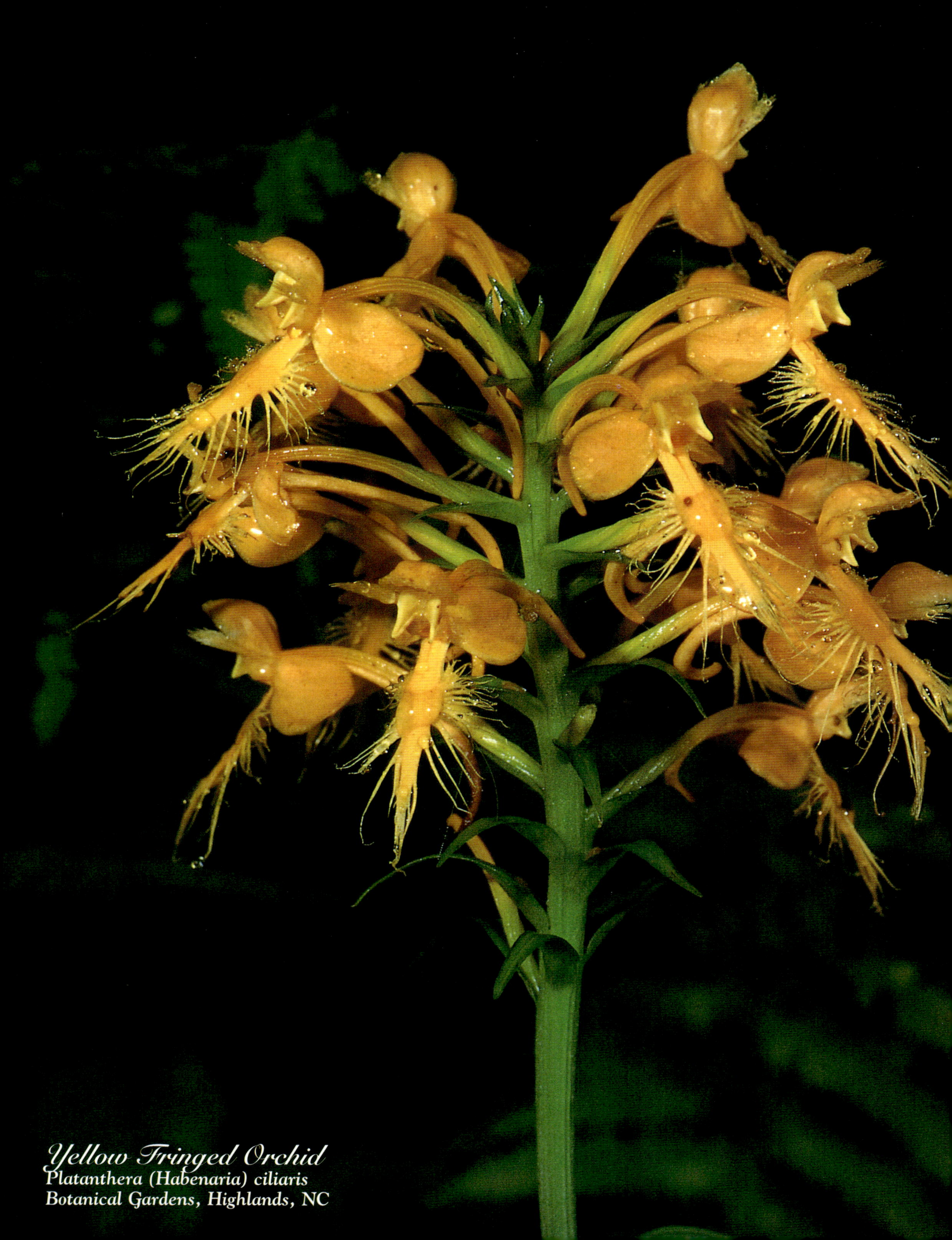

Yellow Fringed Orchid
Platanthera (Habenaria) ciliaris
Botanical Gardens, Highlands, NC

early in the morning when the sunlight was shining through. It was then before my chores began that I liked to skip along the creek banks, searching for the damp areas where violets and lilies grew. We didn't have any neighbors, so I entertained myself combing the woods and collecting wildflowers. I'd pick bunches of violets and pink honeysuckle too. It would make me so happy to take a walk and see one little blooming violet under a log. When I'd see it and examine it, I'd think to myself, how good is God that He's allowed that little purple violet to bloom there for my eyes alone. In my simple childish mind I'd ponder the idea that I was the only person in the world to ever see that violet blooming there under the moss-covered log. It was a marvel to me that God would do such a rare thing for a little girl like me. That He would allow those seeds to be scattered....and the sun to shine, and the April showers too. I could not understand it. It was like a miracle because it was just for me. And I felt such a great sense of joy."

Rudyard Kipling once wrote, "Teach us to delight in simple things." That was Mama...delighting in simple things. We really didn't have to be taught to live simply in those days; for in Mama's generation and mine during the depression, living was nothing but simple in rural Georgia. We had no television, no shopping centers, no money. But we were rich in spirit: we believed in God, His commandments, and our country. There was no class distinction in Pineview; everyone spent their energy trying to survive. The Pineview Bank closed in the crash of 1929, and the rural Georgia farmers lost their life's savings. They had only enough money to put food on their tables and clothe their families. The only people who had an income were a few bootleggers. Most people didn't have a car, and those who did, rarely had electric starters and needed a strong person to go out and hand crank it. Everyone had a huge garden and canned their excess food. They also designed and made clothing for their families.

Hollywood was working on "Gone With The Wind," Roosevelt was making his fireside chats, and Joe Louis was a national hero. We read about Barney Google in the funnies, and I remember the adults talking about Hitler and his invasion of Austria. I had no idea where Austria was, but thought it must be near Atlanta or Cordele, and perhaps his troops would soon reach Pineview, and that would be the end of me. My boundaries were limited, but time was not.

We had time in Pineview to sit on a sack of pecans at the corner drug store and tell stories or listen to the stories of others. We'd swing around the iron poles holding up the tin roof of the Drug Store and the Suwannee Store. Sometimes James, Sammy, Angela and I would go upstairs over the Suwannee Store and play in the old coffins left over from Grandpa Moore's Mercantile store, or slide down James Clements' chicken and storage house tin roof. We'd play hide-and-seek in the bales of cotton in the warehouse. Or spend half of our day scouting around Pineview trying to find someone to take us swimming at Pappy Jack Springs...always beginning with "Crip"

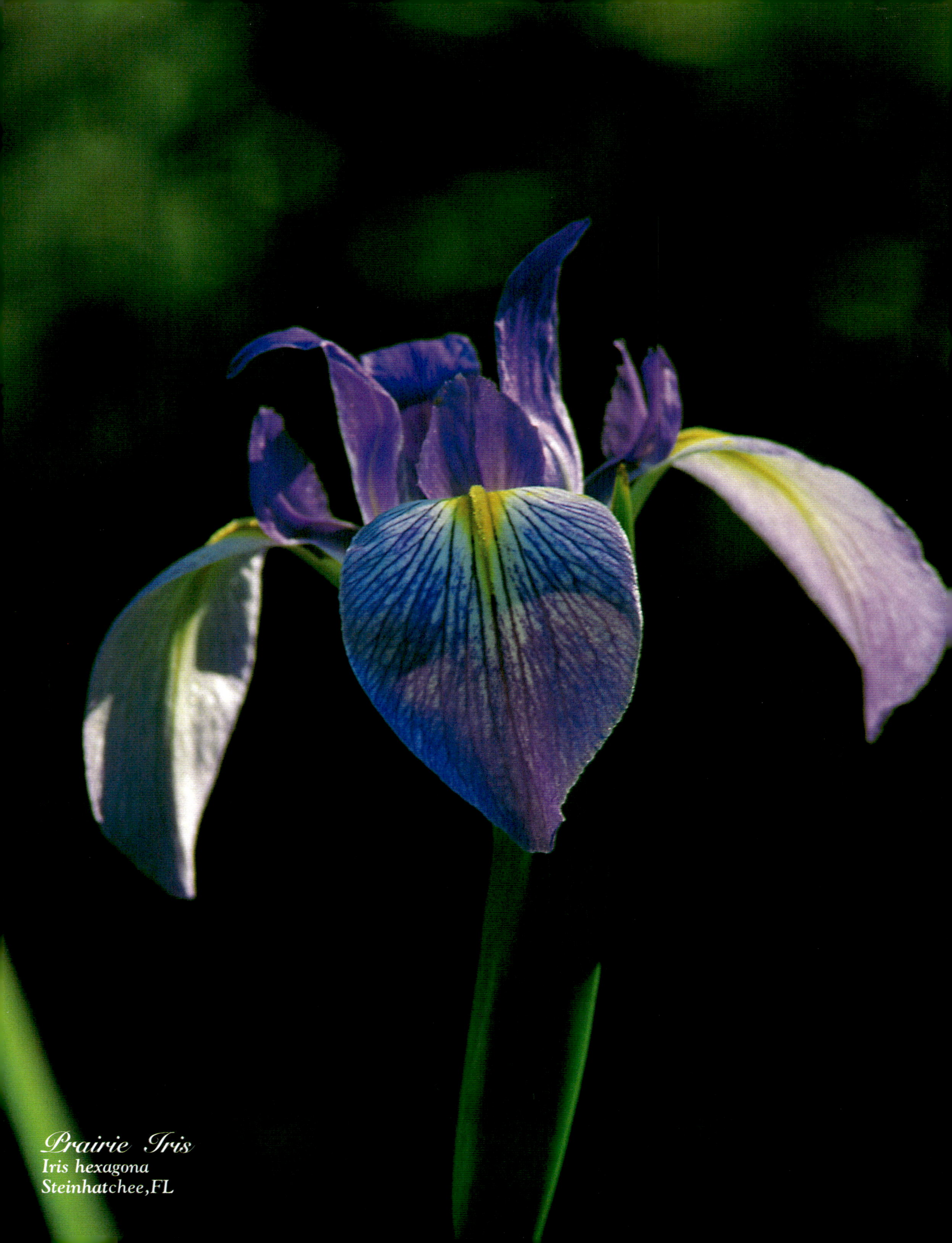

Prairie Iris
Iris hexagona
Steinhatchee,FL

Dennard, who sat on a bench in front of his store playing checkers with his friends. He was an easy target for children. If we succeeded in getting a ride, we'd gather peanuts along the way for boiling or jump a ditch covered with blackberry vines into a field to get a watermelon. Occasionally we'd pick wildflowers with Mama as we did at my sixth birthday party.

The sing-song voices of the children floated back to me across the years. I could see the children's bright eyes as they sang the familiar birthday song while standing around the table with Mama lighting the candles. Angela's laughter rose above the excited voices of the other children when she found the dime Mama had baked in the cake as a surprise. At the end of the day, the only favors the children took home were a fistful of wildflowers and a lasting memory of finding delight in simple beauty hidden in the wild.

The sweet sound of the children's voices was suddenly broken by the scream of jet engines which seemed to be only inches above my head. It jerked my attention toward the sky and away from the happy voices of children and the blue violet at my feet. But even as I moved back into the 1990's and the jet age, I secretly embraced the memory of Mama and the wildflowers and determined that April would always be the month I'd celebrate wildflowers by photographing them. I'd make it a ritual, a part of my life and a part of my nature photography.

Yes, I thought, as I saw my husband walking toward me with the luggage there in the airport, the joy of my sixth birthday was not the gifts the children brought but the gift of a seed planted in my memory of Mama's love of wildflowers.

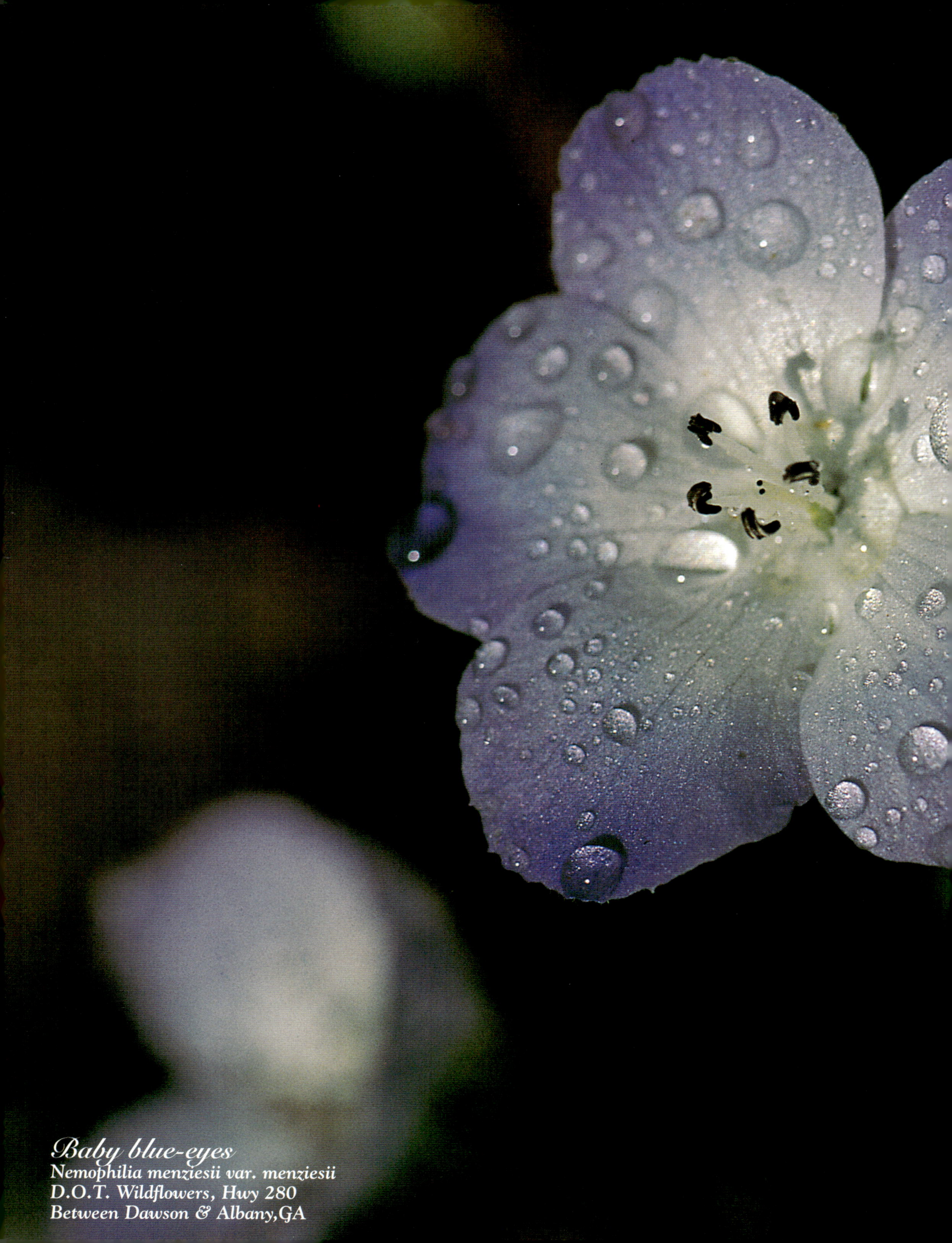

Baby blue-eyes
Nemophilia menziesii var. menziesii
D.O.T. Wildflowers, Hwy 280
Between Dawson & Albany,GA

Divine Seeds

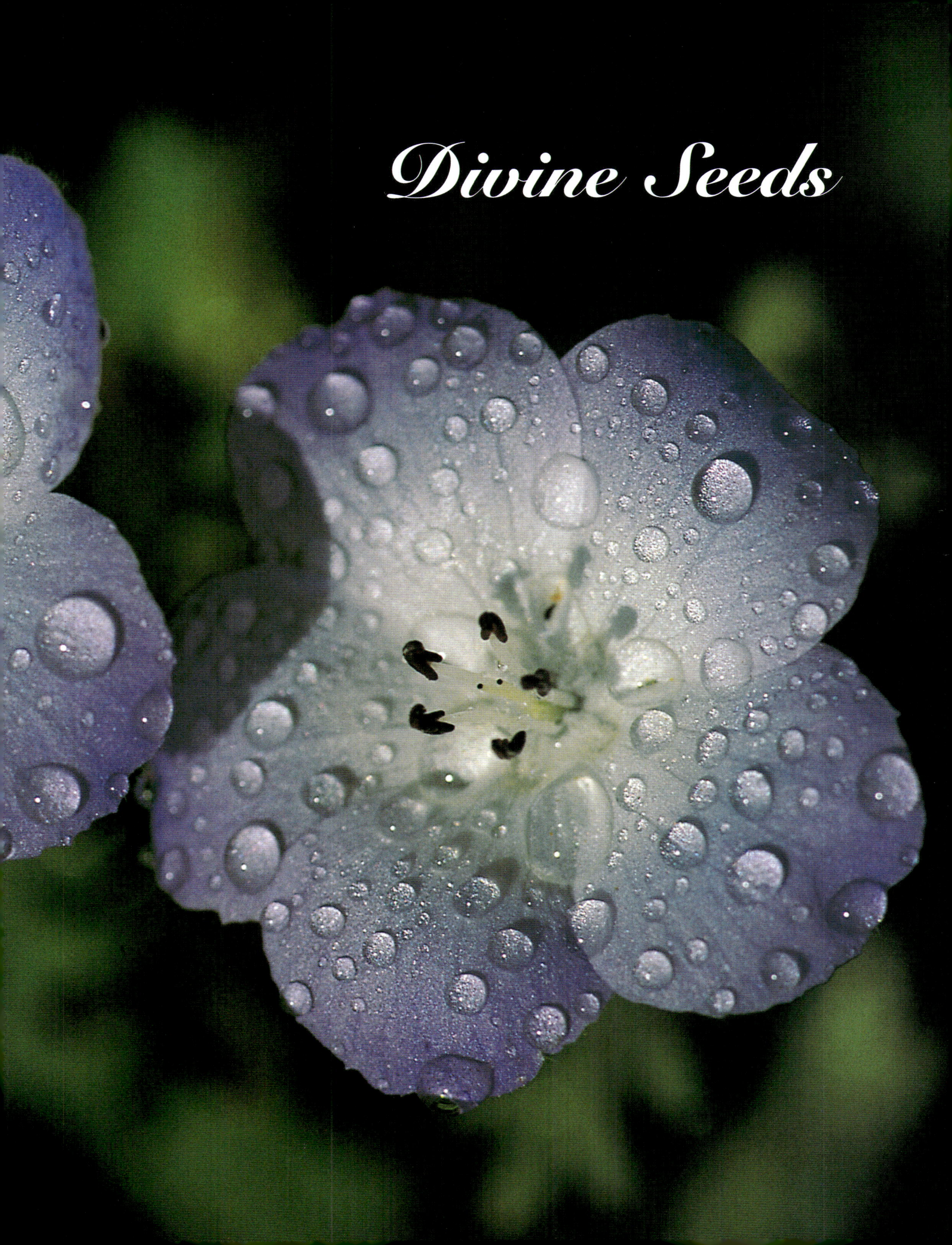

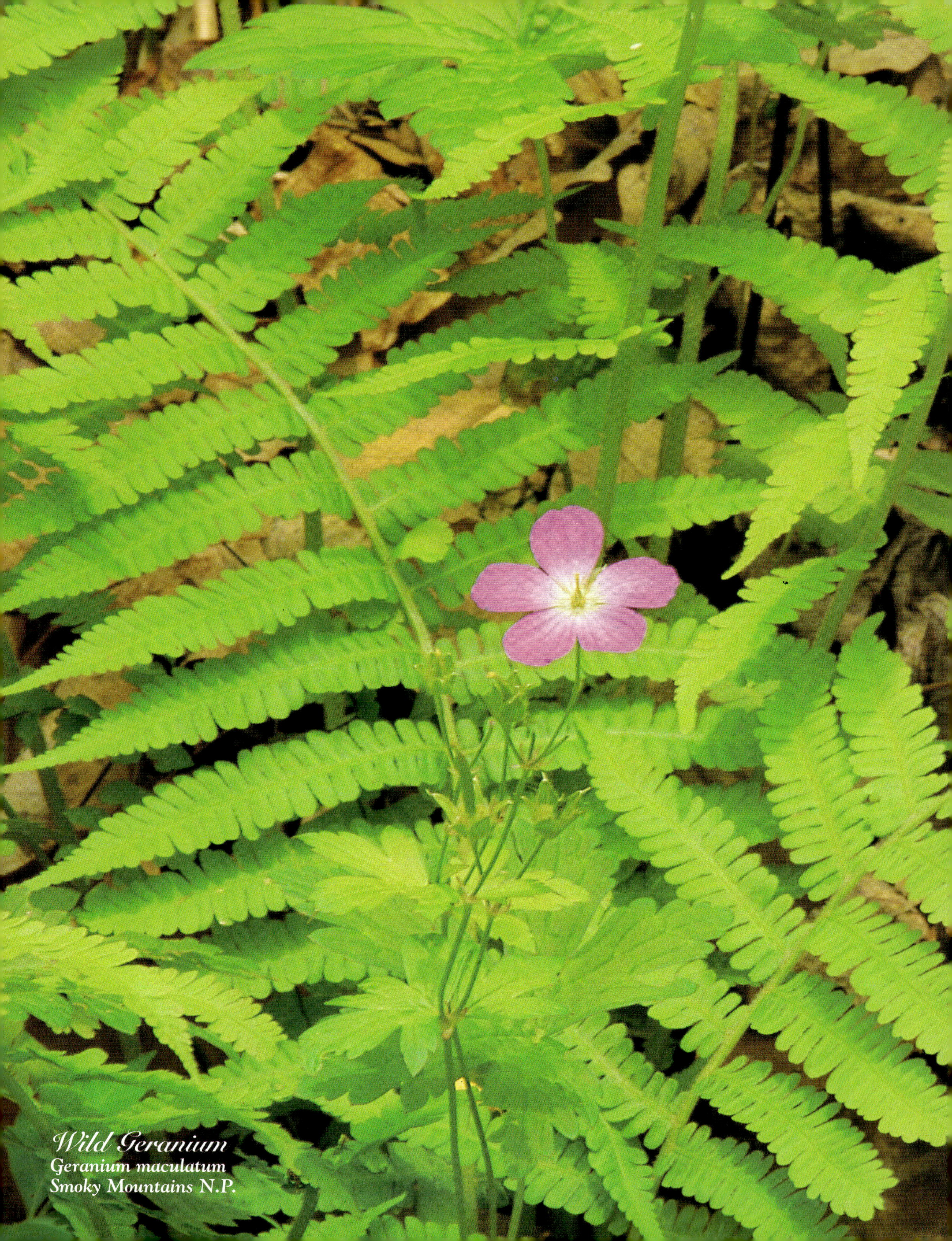

Wild Geranium
Geranium maculatum
Smoky Mountains N.P.

Divine Seeds

"The wild geranium holds its dew
long in the boulder's shade"
William Vaughn Moody

The seed of Mama's love of wildflowers sprouted and grew as I began honoring this wildflower celebration. I developed a greater awareness of their beauty as I passed them growing among the blackberry vines on our southern roadsides. Thinking of gathering more flower images for a book idea, my friend and co-worker, Betty and I, packed the camera equipment in the car one morning. We drove the back country roads from my home in Alabama toward Albany, Georgia to photograph red and orange poppies, blue and pink corn weed, and all sorts of colorful wildflowers.

These particular wildflowers planted in the D.O.T. areas were not native to the Southeast. Even the poppies were from California and not usually found in the area. Bags of mixed wild flower seeds had been brought from Texas where the former president's wife, Lady Bird Johnson, had fallen in love with and created a national interest in wildflowers.

"You know, Betty," I said, as we parked alongside the Dawson-Albany Highway and climbed out of the car, "I remember the days when we had only a few wildflowers growing along the road...maybe some thistles and violets...but they were so small you couldn't see them. There were just a few stray ones here and there. In fact, we didn't even have a paved road then between Pineview and Albany."

"Miz Greene, why were you going to Albany back in those days?" she asked, her face one big smile at the sight of the red and yellow poppies.

"Well, I'd often go along with my Daddy's mother, Grandma Moore, when she visited her sisters and nieces in Albany." I laughed as I went on remembering my cousin telling me about Grandpa Moore's words after his wife's visits to her strong willed family. "Grandpa always said that after one of those trips it took a month to 'get the devil out of Data.' But actually Grandma Moore was very proper and straight laced. I remember her telling me constantly, "Always be a little lady, Honey."

"What other things do you remember about your grandmama?" Betty asked bending down to examine one of the flowers more closely.

"I'd say the one thing I recall most about her was her strength. She taught me to be strong, too. She gave me a kind of insight into myself that I couldn't have gotten anywhere else. Since I was born in Grandma Moore's old Victorian house, and my family and I lived with her during the depression, whenever my aunts brought my cousins to visit I felt that I was on my home turf, and that the cousins were the visitors.

"I betcha' she woulda' made you behave if she was like my Grandmama," Betty laughed.

"You're right," I chuckled. " She was the strong disciplinarian in my life and always kept a switch nearby in case she needed it. But she was a gentle and caring person too. I'll always be grateful for her taking me to get my eyes examined and making sure I got the glasses I needed. I heard that she often helped her neighbors when they had babies or an illness in their families. Daddy said she gave wandering Creek Indians food when he was a little boy. Maybe that was because she couldn't forget the hunger she'd experienced as a three-year-old at the end of the Civil War.

"You mean she was living then...in the Civil War?" Betty asked incredulously.

"Yes, I didn't realize it either until Roy and I were visiting her a few months after our marriage. She was almost one hundred years old then. We were sitting in the rockers on her back porch when she started telling us the story about Sherman marching his troops to Savannah and stopping at her house.

As I told Betty the story, I could almost hear Grandma Moore's voice: "Since our young men, even the teenagers, were off in the army and not around to help us, our food supply was real low. We had only a few canned goods, and the apples and peaches were still drying on the front porch. Sherman's men built a large fire in our yard and burned everything we had including the dried fruit. I was only three years old," she said, "but I still remember." Turning in her rocker she looked Roy in the eye and asked, "Son, you're not a Yankee are you?"

"She was only three years old but it made such a lasting impression on her," I told Betty, "as it would any child. That's probably the reason she was so frugal and saving."

"What did she look like? " Betty asked.

"It's funny, but when I think of her now, I always see her in the same black and white print dress, wearing a black, small-brimmed hat. I know she had other types of clothes because Mama said when she was a young woman Grandma Moore wore the latest style and liked to put things together to give herself a 'snappy' look. But that's the picture I have of her."

"She must have been a lot different from your mom," Betty remarked.

"You can say that again," I told her. I unscrewed the legs of the high tripod and began pushing the extensions in to get a shorter length. The flowers were still wet with dew, and a few trucks were beginning to pass on the highway. "She was a stern, direct, no-nonsense person," I continued. "People called her bossy, but with all of us living there in her home, I guess she needed to be bossy to get anything done."

I walked over to look at the flowers from a different angle. Their bright colors lifted my spirit as we continued our conversation. "Yes," I said, "there was a big contrast between Grandma Moore and Mama. When I was with Mama and her family

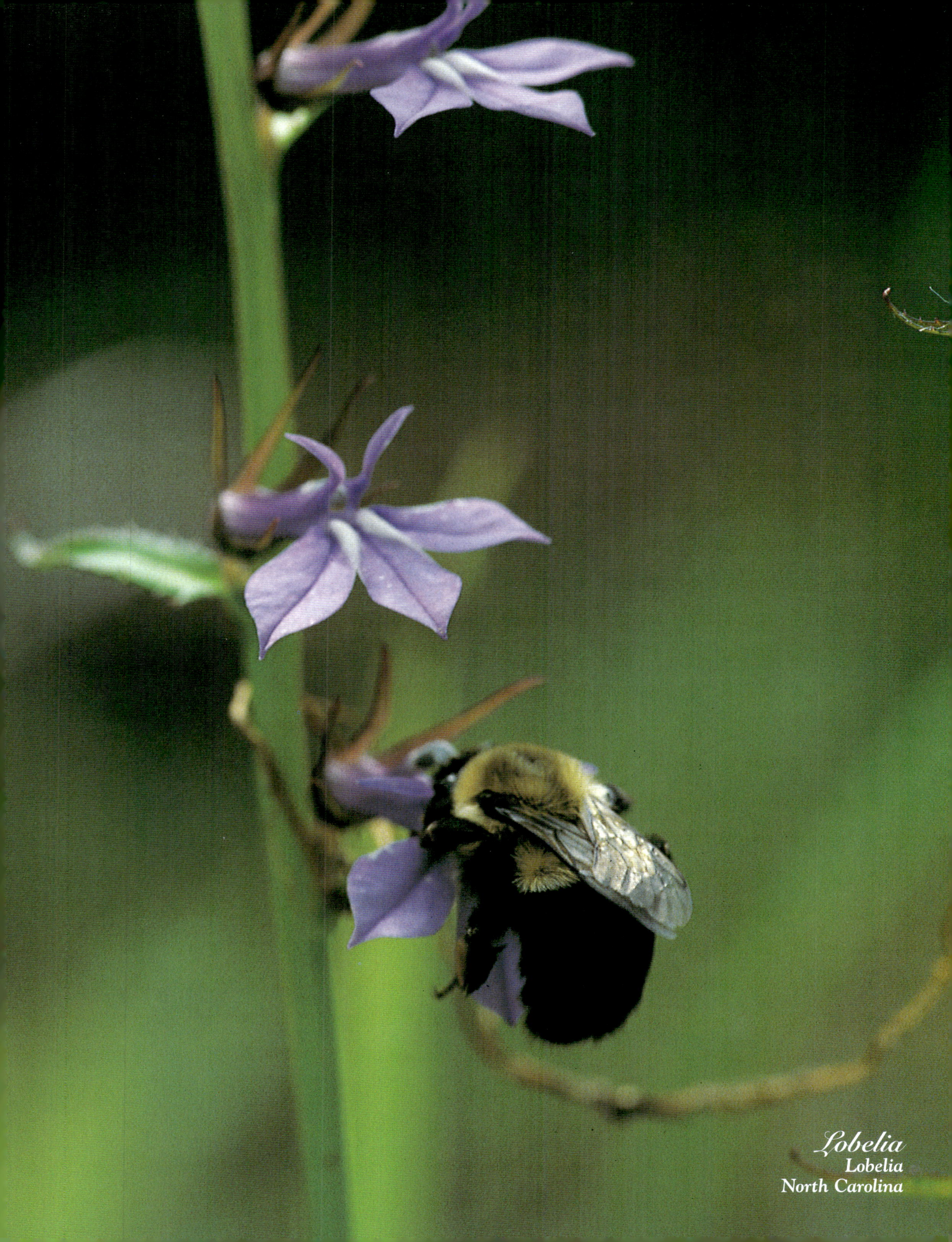

Lobelia
Lobelia
North Carolina

we were always laughing and telling funny stories. But I can see now that those years of strong discipline with Grandma Moore were good for me too. I can even appreciate the part of her in me today that makes me outspoken and direct in my speech. Roy often tells me I'm just like Data, but at least I'm not afraid to speak the truth. And I do have a pretty strong sense of responsibility...too much sometimes...just like Grandma."

Getting down on my knees and peering through the viewfinder, I felt as old as Grandma Moore always looked to me. But even though she was old, she still worked in her vegetable garden. Often, she'd dig around her rose bushes near the front porch too. I remembered swinging there on the porch with my brother, David, watching people drag their long cotton bags through the open fields of white cotton. We'd swing high over the large low-growing hydrangeas that surrounded the house as the scent of the sweet shrub bushes mingled with the pungent smell of dew-covered cotton. He and I often played in her front yard, climbed the Magnolia trees and rode bareback on our pony, Stonewall, while she cut roses in the early morning.

Sitting there on the Albany highway with Betty, a garden of wildflowers spread before us, I was reminded of another day in the 1930's when I was riding down a similar road north of Albany with Grandma Moore and her brother, Uncle "T." As usual we'd spent the day with their sister in Albany and were traveling back to Pineview. I was a little girl sitting low in the back seat of Grandma's black stick-shift Plymouth with the tin-covered spare tire on the back. It started raining after we'd left, and Grandma and Uncle "T" were worried that we might not make it home because the clay roads were getting wet and slippery. The red bow in my sunbleached bobbed hair, as bright as the red poppies on the highway, bounced in rhythm with the car movement on the bumpy roads. Looking at my favorite book, *Goldilocks And the Three Bears*, I could smell the dusty seat covers and feel the scratchy fabric on my bare legs. Uncle 'T' was driving pretty fast when suddenly I felt the car slip and slide. I jumped up in the back seat to see what was happening, but by that time the car had spun completely around, and we were turned in the opposite direction, headed back to Albany.

"Whoaaa!" I cried. "What's happening, Uncle T ....?"

Gripping the steering wheel with both hands, he was too busy to answer. But through it all, his white head never bobbled, and his bow tie stayed steady around his neck. He continued to drive on as though nothing unusual had happened, staring straight ahead, trying to hold the car in the red ruts. Clutching the back of Grandma's seat, I looked over to see what she was going to do. Instead of exploding or yelling with fright, she just said calmly, "'T', don't you think you'd better turn back around and head for Pineview?" That was Grandma Moore: calm, matter-of-fact, and in control even when things around her weren't.

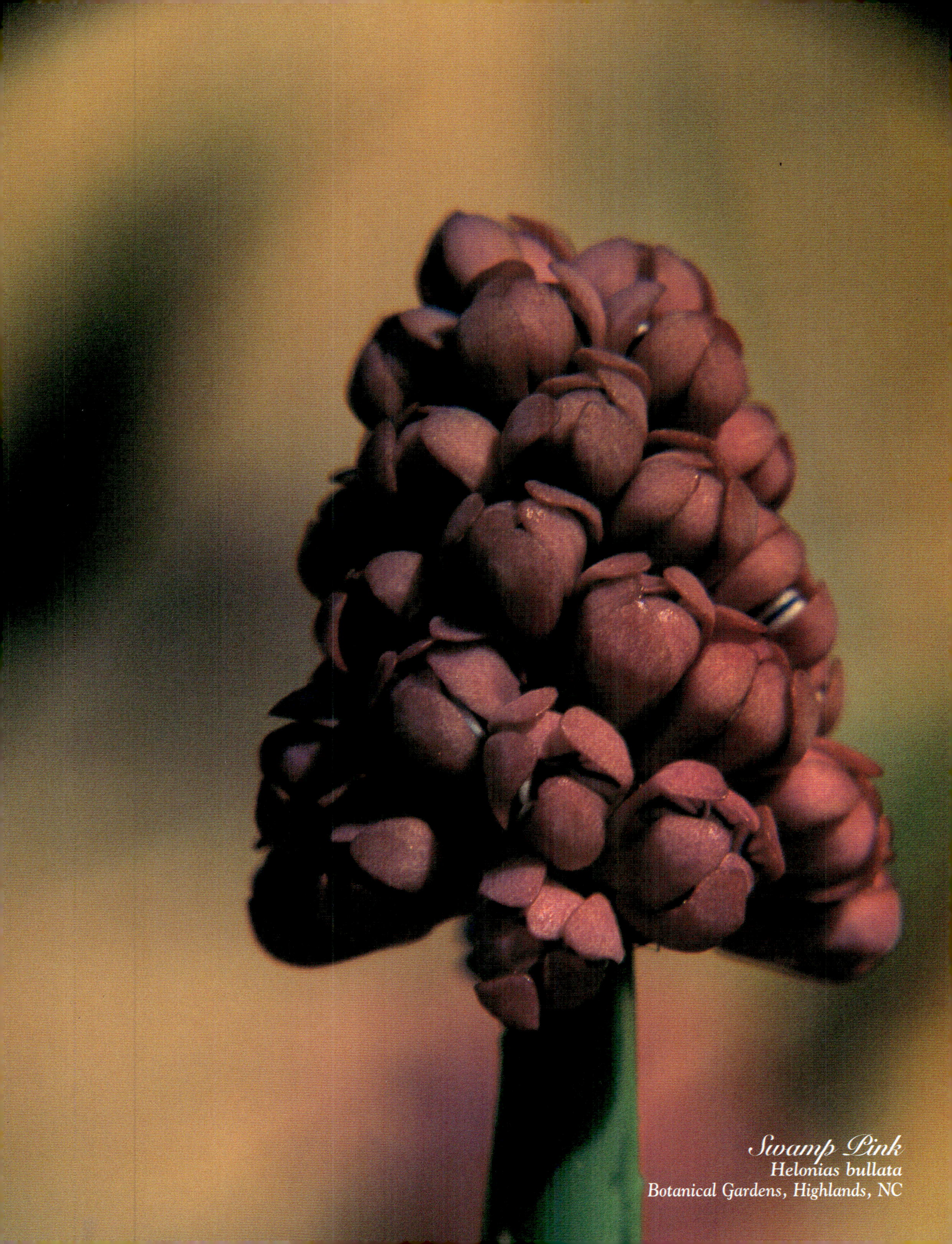

Swamp Pink
Helonias bullata
Botanical Gardens, Highlands, NC

Feeling the warm Georgia sun on my shoulders, I focused the camera lens on a big red poppy with its black center. I was still amazed at the hundreds of wildflowers in front of me. There were probably more wildflowers in those depression days, too, I thought, but most people called them weeds. My mama was the only one I knew who saw them as flowers. "A wildflower has a freedom of spirit," Mama said. "They grow willingly wherever their seeds are scattered and are never forced in hot houses." That's the way Grandma's spirit was: unrestrained, not cultivated or forced into certain patterns by anyone but God. She could have been considered a weed by some, I thought. She was so independent, so capable of pushing through any circumstance or barrier to come out strong on the other side. But there was also a beauty in the way she accepted so much responsibility that still drew me to her after all those years. It's just the way you look at things, I thought, that makes you see them as "weeds" or "wildflowers."

I felt a breeze from a big truck as it rumbled by on the highway. As I waited for the windblown flowers to settle down, Betty asked, "Aren't you afraid to come out here and take these pictures?"

I smiled as she moved quickly off the road. "No, I'm not," I said. "I guess it's just more of Grandma's genes running through me. Even when I was little, my brother and friends in Pineview would push me out front when they were afraid. Maybe that's why I don't back away from things today."

"Yeah," Betty said, "I didn't even know your Grandma Moore, but from what you tell me, I can see her out here photographing these wildflowers on the side of the road ... or going off to the Everglades to find wading birds, if that's what she wanted to do. It was like she put your feet firm down into the ground," Betty said.

"That's it exactly," I said. "She must have contributed to the part of me that makes me feel grounded... maybe it's because I felt so sure of myself there at her house, the place where I was born, where I lived, learned and played during my early years. I always felt like I belonged and was accepted in whatever I did."

I sat down on a nearby rock and waited for the right light. "It's like the seeds of my being were born there in the yard of that old house. You'll probably laugh at this, Betty," I said, "but when I dream about that place today, I sometimes dream of lions and tigers and leopards....all animals of great strength, walking around the Magnolia trees in Grandma Moore's yard. I guess it's because it was there that I knew I was on my surest ground, the place where I grew like the wildflowers grow, and I know now that wherever I go, I take Grandma Moore's yard with me."

Yes, I thought, as Betty and I began loading the equipment into the car. I find that same feeling in my nature photography, that sureness of being on solid ground. Photographing the flowers offers me a chance to spend some quiet moments in the ground of my own being. It gives me that greater awareness and sense of self I often long for, but seldom take time to realize is already there for me to draw upon. When I sit with my camera in hand, focusing on the wildflowers, their fragrance and vibrant colors help me expand; they touch my soul. They ground me like Grandma Moore's front yard.

Everyone needs a special grounding place to grow the seeds of their potential. Macrina Wiederkehr once wrote, "The seeds sown in our lives are, in reality, seeds of our potential. They are sparks of the Divine. They must take root in the earthiness of our lives and grow." I know now that we, too, must be grounded if we are to eventually bloom like the wildflowers.

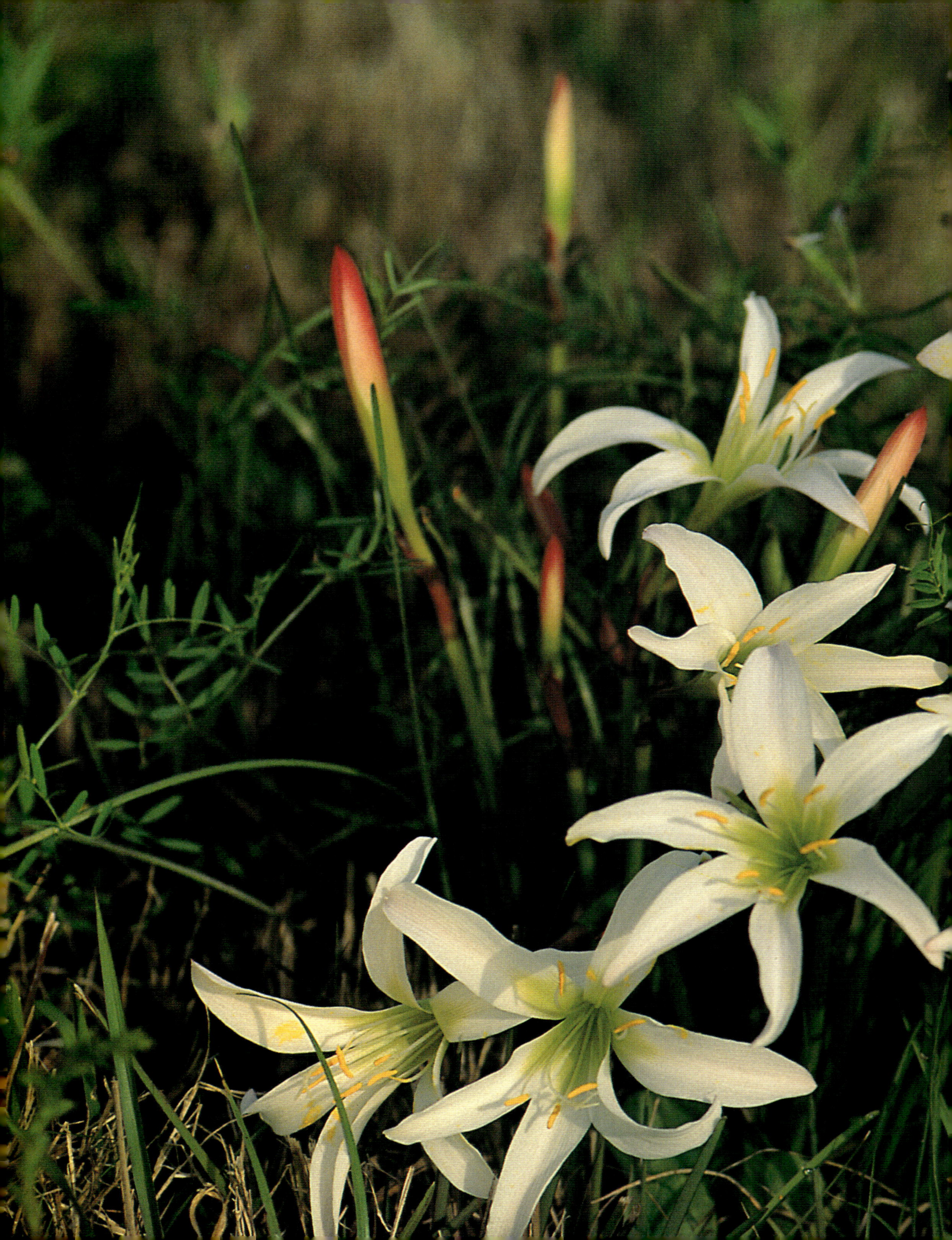

Earth's Jewels

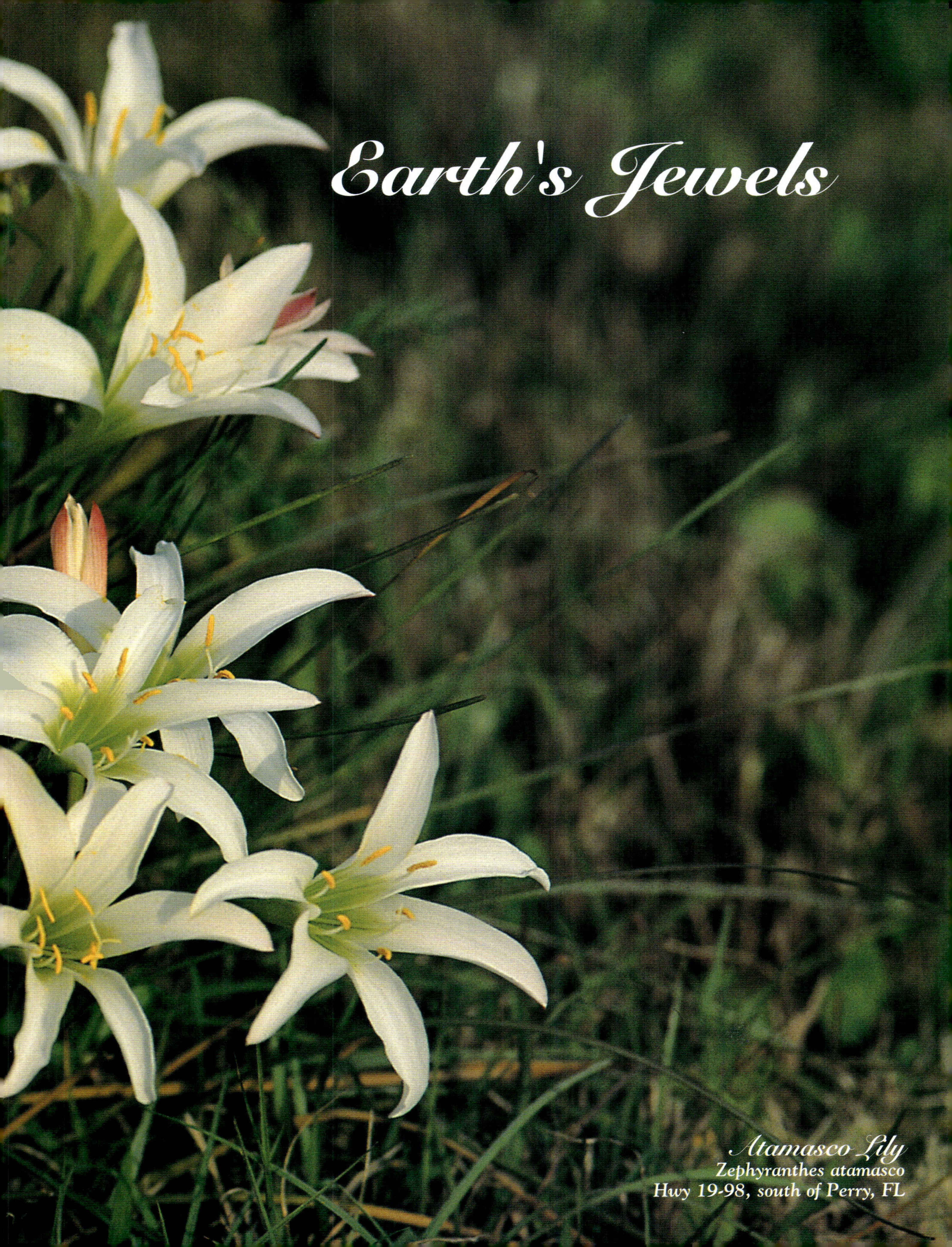

Atamasco Lily
Zephyranthes atamasco
Hwy 19-98, south of Perry, FL

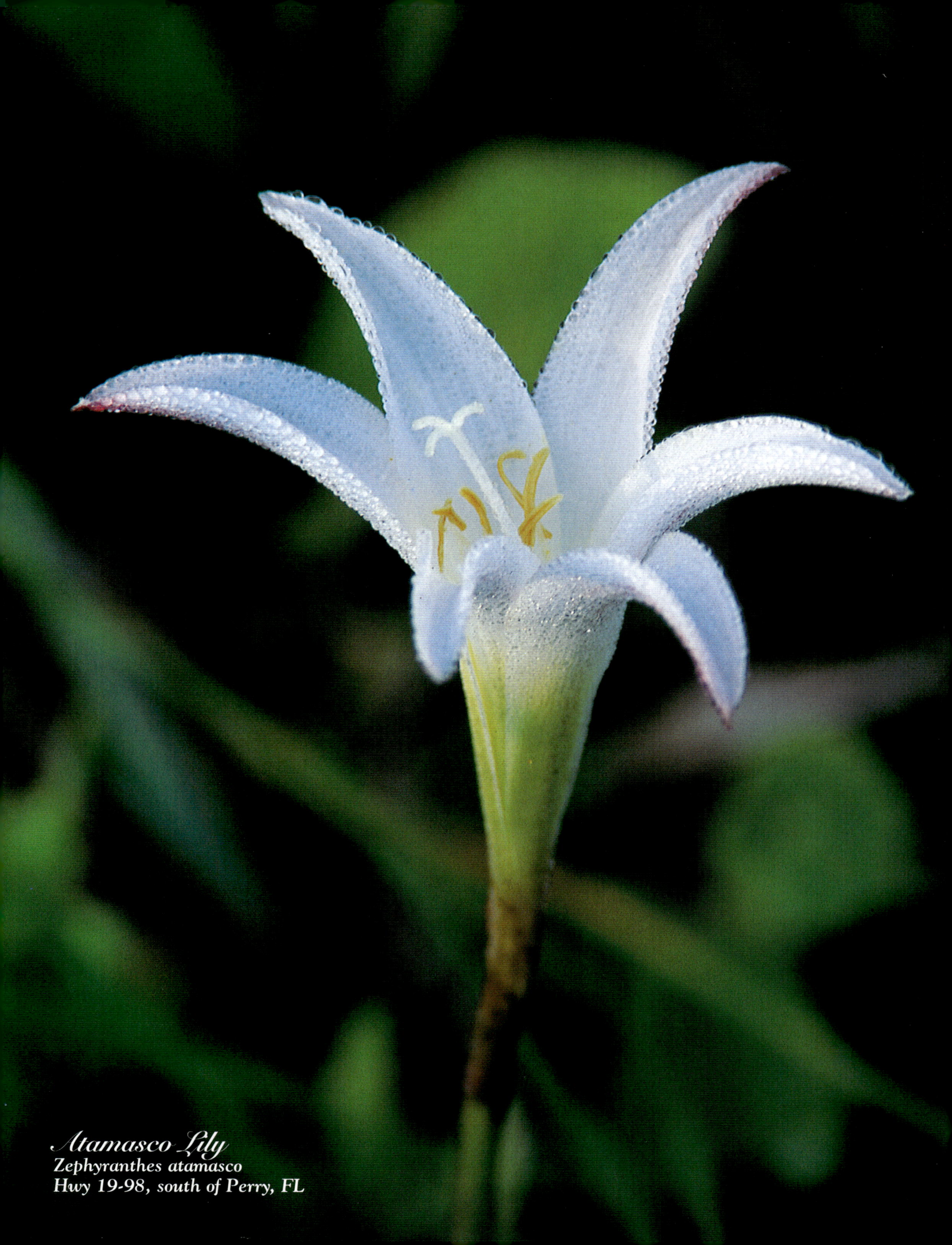

Atamasco Lily
Zephyranthes atamasco
Hwy 19-98, south of Perry, FL

Earth's Jewels

To see a world in a grain of sand
And a heaven in a wildflower;
Hold infinity in the palm of your hand,
And eternity in an hour.
William Blake

I valued the treasures of Mama's love of wildflowers and having a special grounding place even more one summer as I stood on a smelly old boat dock with tears in my eyes. Our ten-year search for a retirement dream house had ended at an ancient wholesale fish house. I couldn't believe my husband Roy had bought the old commercial building. It was sitting only a few feet from the street, directly across from the Baptist Church on the Steinhatchee River. The road sign's black dangling letters matched my spirit as I stared at the end of my dream.

"Why did you buy this?" I asked. "What can you mean?"

"Janie, I'll fix it up, and it will make a pretty vacation house overlooking the river."

"But we wanted a place that overlooked the ocean," I said.

"This is only a mile from the ocean," he replied. "Besides it's got a deep water dock, and I can put my boat here."

"You don't need a deep dock for your boat...you don't have a sailboat, anymore. You sold it."

"Well, I'll get another one," he answered.

"I don't like it. In fact, I can't stand it! I hate it!" I cried.

"You can hate it, but I'm going to build a house here," he said. Roy was a person who walked to the beat of his own drummer and was in solid control of his destiny. Furthermore, he was always going on a new adventure! He took what Walt Whitman called the open road. "Afloat and light-hearted, I take to the open road. Healthy, free, the world before me. The Long brown path before me leading wherever I choose."

Before he gave me the special viewing of his fish house, he showed it to his nephew's young friend, Jim. When he saw it, Jim shook his head in disbelief..."I don't think so, Uncle Roy."

"Don't you think Janie can use her imagination and make this place look good, Jim?" he asked.

He shook his head and said, "Uncle Roy, Aunt Janie will have to use a whole lot more than imagination to fix this place up."

But, Roy used HIS imagination. He re-designed and rebuilt the house. According to the building inspector, he had to keep the bathroom in the same place as the original fish house. It mattered little to Roy that the bathroom was just off the kitchen. I helped him select his living room furniture and made a few suggestions on

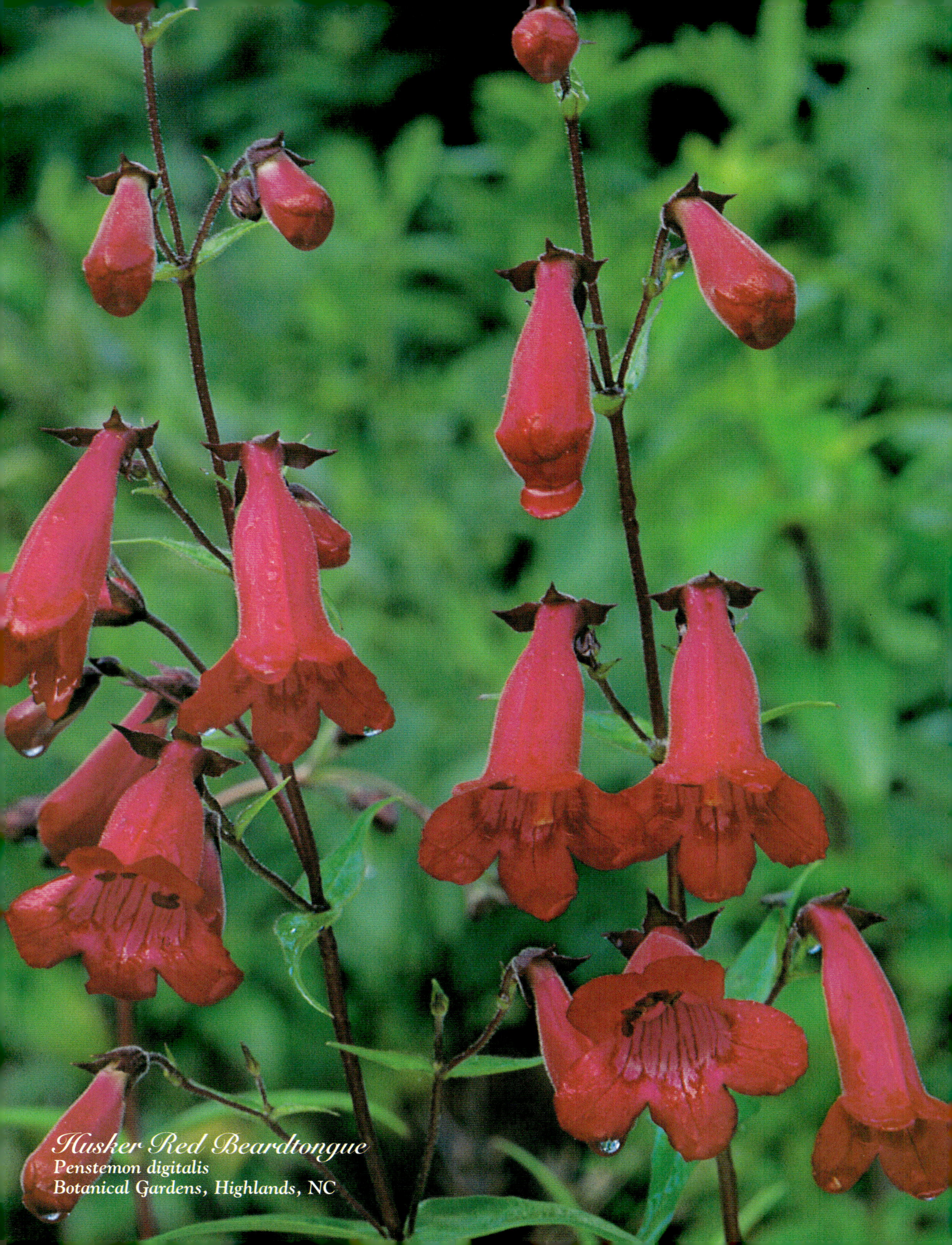

Husker Red Beardtongue
Penstemon digitalis
Botanical Gardens, Highlands, NC

the construction of the building, but the rest was all his masculine creation, his retreat house. He liked it that way.

It was not, however, the place I wanted to spend my retirement years. I loved roses and wildflowers and beautiful, graceful wading birds and white beaches and blue oceans and sailboats skimming by. I liked nature photography and solitude, not the sounds of cars passing my bedroom at night. Standing there with Roy that day, all I could see were rusty tin roofs, trailers, and old, old unpainted boat docks and buildings with rotten boards, most of which served as vacation houses for fishermen.

I didn't want a river house at Steinhatchee, but he continued building. He installed double doors to open out on a screen porch that overlooked an island of palm trees and live oaks and pine. Often we'd see an eagle resting on one of the limbs of an old dead oak. His building project lasted more than a year.

With my camera, I'd sometimes drive down with him to fish and check on his house. Along the way we would see colorful wildflowers beside the drainage ditches and on both sides of the road right-of-ways. We'd also see lovely feathered wading birds moving between green and lilac lily pads. But, several months into his building project, the Storm of the Century hit the Steinhatchee River and raised the tide seventeen feet high. With the combination of high tides and the wind-blown waves, practically every dock and house was damaged along the river. I regretted that the people there lost so much of their property. However, I was secretly disappointed that the storm failed to wash away the fish house marquee advertising a cut rate for mullet fish which still stood at an angle in front of my future vacation house.

By the time Roy had finished remodeling his house, many of the residents had rebuilt their vacation houses and boat docks back along the winding river. They'd painted their houses, restaurants, and other buildings. Most of Steinhatchee looked brand new!

After Roy had repaired the old rotten and storm-damaged boat dock, he bought an airboat and invited me to go fishing. I liked to fish for red-fish and trout, so I gladly tagged along. We went with John, a Steinhatchee fisherman, who encouraged Roy to buy the lot and the boat. The loud plane-like motor roared as it floated above the water shallows and saw-grass. We surprised huge flocks of White Egrets, Great Blue Herons, and Snowy Egrets. I was enthralled with the natural beauty. Roy grinned knowingly as he handed me ear phones to muffle out the loud noise of the engine. John drove us through lake-like shallows to see a flock of sixty or more white Ibis. Then we rounded an island and saw forty or fifty white pelicans. I had no camera and couldn't photograph them, but my heart and mind recorded them in a lasting memory. We watched hundreds of birds feeding in the shallows and flying low beside us almost touching the surface of the cool water. I felt like a dancer moving on the music of violins as we floated above the water that Spring day.

We drove through the birds for an hour before we found John's "honey pot" of a fishing hole in a narrow creek surrounded by red, green and sand-colored saw-grass. We caught one red-fish after another. It was a great day!

I thought to myself that Audubon, the 19th century nature artist, had never experienced a day like the one that was ours that morning. We saw more of nature's bounty in one hour's drive on the airboat than he'd seen in years of paddling his canoe and sketching birds.

I got up early the next morning, awakened by a dream of picking up beautiful jeweled emerald and diamond bracelets and necklaces from the sand. They were everywhere I looked! Still groggy from the deep sleep, I dressed and left the cabin before my fisherman husband got up. I'd spotted some white Easter Lilies blooming along the road as we drove to Steinhatchee the day before; and I wanted to photograph them while the morning dew was still on them. Carefully, I drove along the four lane highway searching for the few remaining lilies the mowers hadn't cut down. I finally found a clump of five or six.

The sun was rising as I dragged my tripod and camera from the car and set it up next to the clump of lilies. Lowering the tripod directly in front of the lilies only inches from the ground, I slid the camera onto the quick release plate. Then I twisted in the macro lens and focused on a single white lily with its yellow stamin. Looking through the viewfinder, I saw hundreds of shining dew drops clinging to the sides of each white lily petal. The tiny, sparkling liquid drops jumped out at me and I caught my breath at the exquisite jewel-like beauty magnified through the lens of the camera.

Resting for a moment from my lotus-like position on the ground, the truth of my early morning dream hit me! I was not picking up emeralds and diamond bracelets from the sand; I was picking up beautiful photographs of gorgeous jewel-covered wildflowers from the Florida sand....jewels from the earth. Yes, I thought, all wildflowers are exquisite jewels from the earth....a treasure waiting to be discovered! I thought of how God blesses us with millions of such jewels each day, and we're not even aware of them. We walk or drive past them. We step on them. We even mow them down. I knew I'd enjoyed being in the wildflowers too long. Roy was waiting to go fishing; so gathering the tri-pod and cameras, I put them back into the car and climbed in.

As I was driving back to Roy's fish camp, the memory of the Broadway musical "*Mame*" floated into my mind. I could hear the music as she sang, "Open the window, travel a new highway......." I thought of my adventuresome husband and laughed. Roy and Mame would have made great companions. But perhaps even I could open the window just a crack and learn to appreciate traveling on new highways.

Then I passed the huge billboard pointing to Steinhatchee. "In the heart of the THE NATURE COAST", it read. Wasn't that my interest now? Exploring nature with my camera? Here around Steinhatchee was the perfect place to photograph southern birds and wildflowers. So acting on Mame's advice, I slowly opened the window just a little more and felt the warm breeze blowing. Maybe, just maybe, I was exactly where I was supposed to be, and just maybe too, Steinhatchee wasn't so bad after all!

Yes, I mused as I rounded the curve to the cabin. I would travel the new highway with my adventuresome husband and appreciate all that my life touched along the way. I could hear Mame singing, "Live, live, live! Life is a banquet, and most poor suckers are starving to death." No, I thought, I won't starve anymore...not with this banquet of life before me!

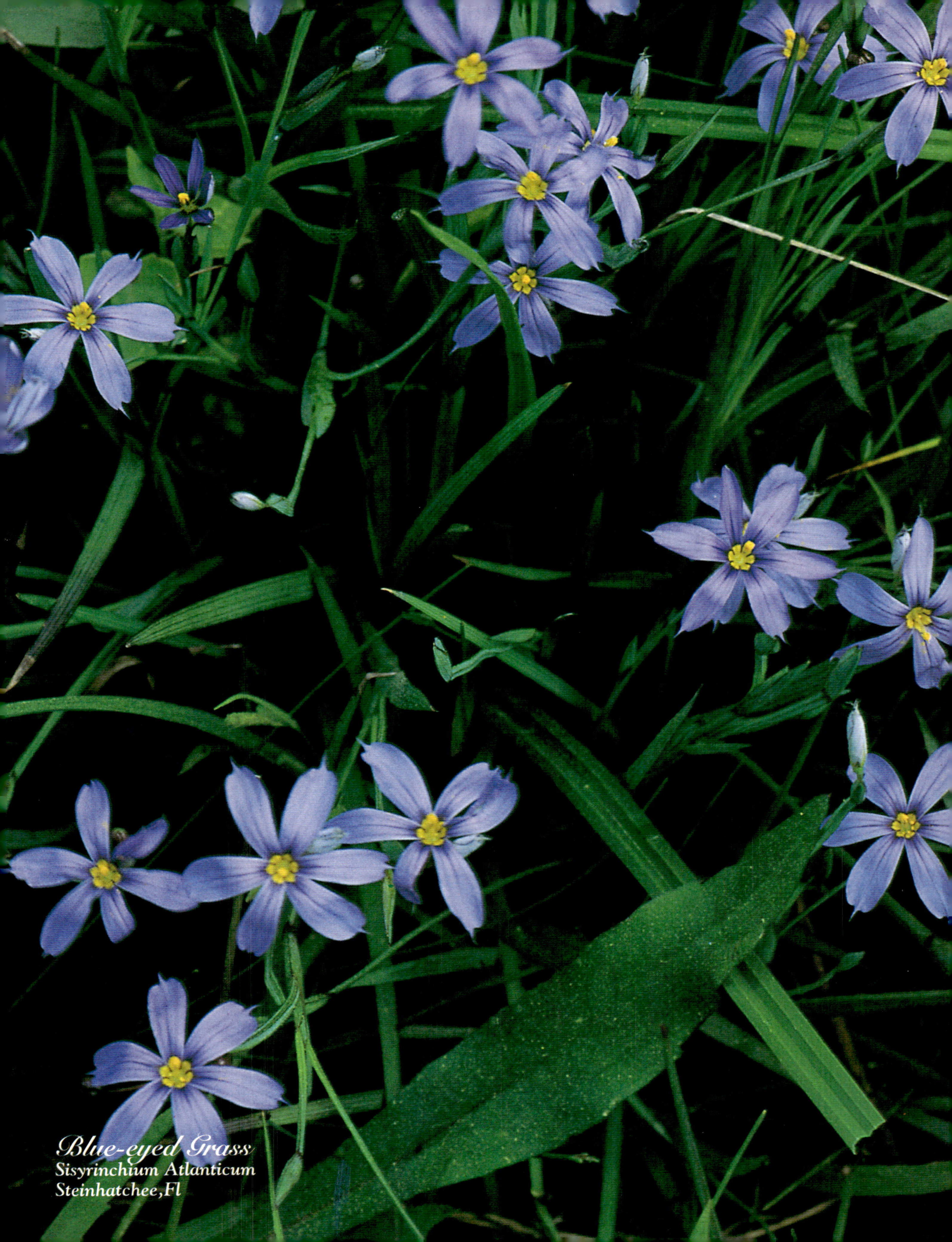

Blue-eyed Grass
Sisyrinchium Atlanticum
Steinhatchee,Fl

Let the Dance Begin

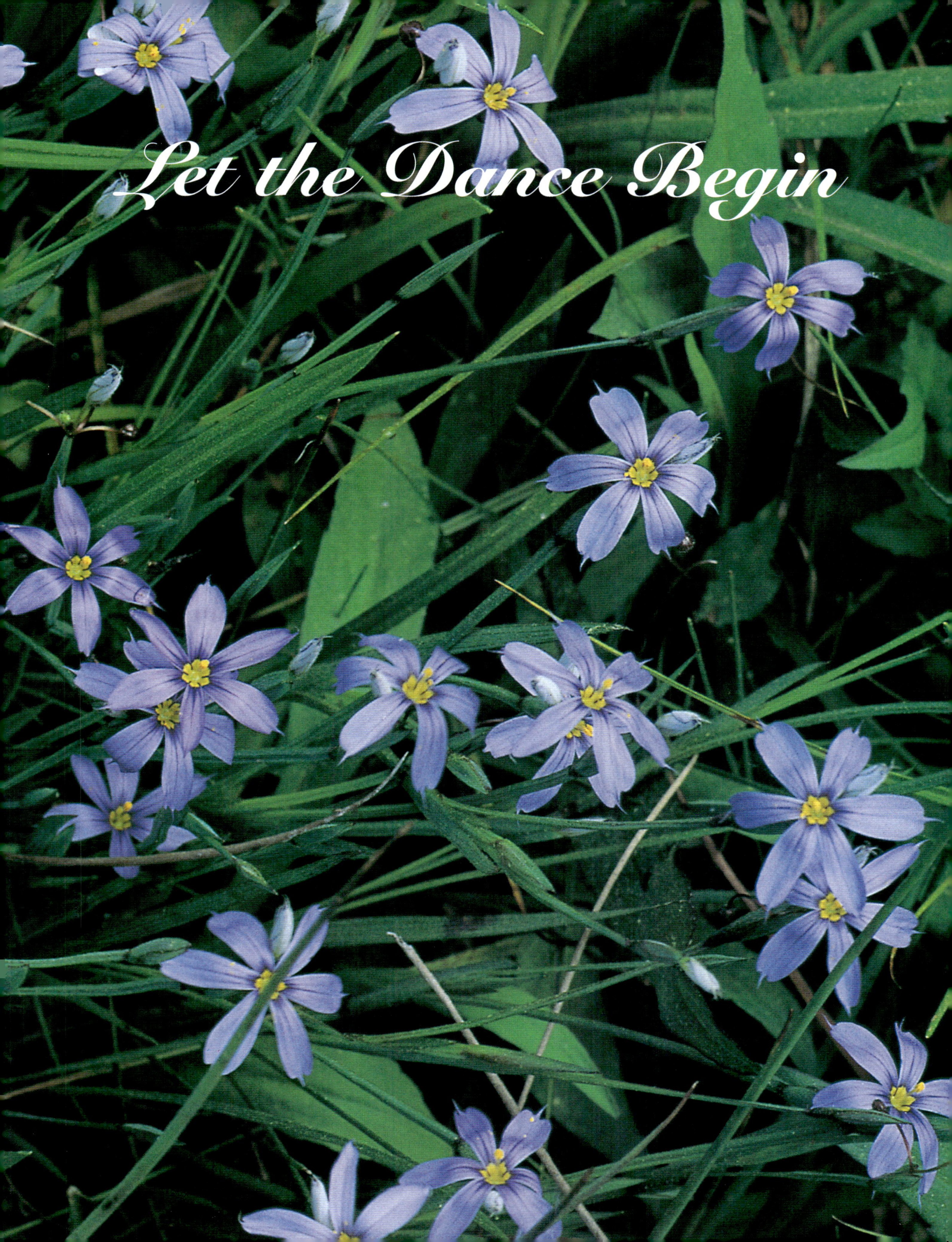

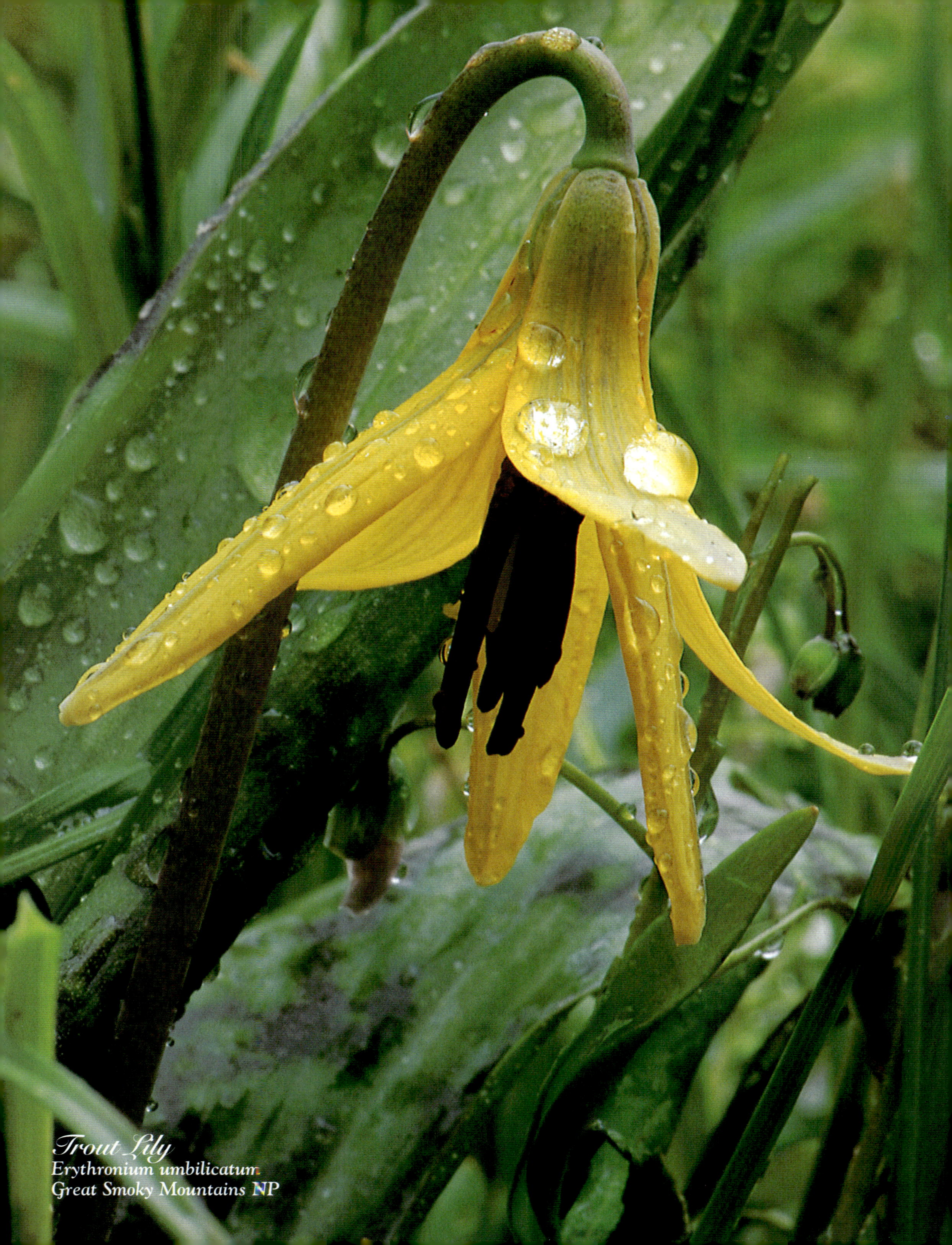

Trout Lily
Erythronium umbilicatum
Great Smoky Mountains NP

Let the Dance Begin

For lo, the winter is past,
the rain is over and gone.
The flowers appear on the earth,
The time of singing has come.
Song of Solomon 2:11-12 Holy Bible RSV

The diarist Anais Nin once wrote, “The days when I am happiest are the days when I hear music in everything.” That’s the way it was for me one March morning when Betty and I went to Callaway Gardens to look for Trout Lilies. Flowers danced against their winter brown backdrop to the tune of a brown thrasher singing his heart out from the top of a Cherry Tree. Raindrops clung to the petals as though it were their last hope for the season, and I felt like dancing myself, twirling, whirling among those first wildflowers of the year.

The little yellow dots sprinkled about on the green carpet of grass heralded Spring. They were bravely defying the heavy frost expected that night. I whispered to myself, “Let the dance begin.” Dancing to me was far more joyful than simply hearing the music.

Betty, agreed to go with me to help carry the tripod and hold the reflector so I could get extra light on the wildflowers. We saw Trout Lily buds here and there as we walked along beside the rushing stream, but none of them were open. As we searched through the dark woods for other lilies, we talked about her children and mine. Betty’s husband, Junior, had died the year before and she felt the responsibility for decision making in her family. She told me about her daughter Loretta leaving college to join the army.

“You haven’t mentioned that, Betty.” I said.

“Oh yes..., my son “May-May” called me the other day, and said, “Mama, I’m gonna’ take you over to Montgomery to see Loretta. She wants us to come.” So I went over there with him, and I nearly fainted, Miz Greene. She was standing there with a little green army cap sitting at an angle on her head. She said she was jus’ gonna’ surprise me.”

“What did you say, Betty?” I asked.

“I’m not gonna’ tell you what I said, but when I saw her standing there with that little cap on, it shocked me to death. I kinda’ froze for a minute! I thought I was gonna’ go berserk! To tell you the truth, I said something terrible, ... but I calmed down when she explained it to me. She’d got “May-May” to come bring me to Montgomery because she didn’t know what I’d say or do. I didn’t even know she’d joined the army. I ain’t never been so surprised except when I saw those birds with you that day in the bird rookery when you were working on the other book.”

Suddenly Betty stopped talking and pointed to the side of the path. "Here are some more lilies," she said, motioning toward an almost indistinguishable group, "and there's a blossom! I never have paid attention to these flowers before, Miz Greene," she said bending down to get a closer look. "They're real pretty."

Our joy was short-lived for the lilies had been bruised by the rain and I couldn't use them. However, off to the side, we spotted some Anemones scattered along a small hillside. A touch of pink splashed across their white faces. We would have missed them if we had not stopped for the rain-bruised lilies.

Nearby, red-breasted robins strutted around as though they could hardly wait for the fullness of Spring. The limbs of deciduous trees were so bare they were almost depressing. The air was turning cooler by that time, and I began to worry about Betty who had left her jacket at home. Her blue silk blouse didn't look as if it were warm enough for the wintry front that was moving in, but she brushed aside my reservations as she got down on her knees to see if the reflector would project more light on the Anemones.

I placed the tripod on the wet earth beside her as the two of us began one of the early tasks of trying to create a new book. "It has to begin somewhere, Betty," I said, "so it might as well be here." I put the camera in a plate on top of the tripod and unfolded the three legs to get the camera closer to the earth and the spreading Anemones. Grunting with every lowered inch, I was aware that I had not photographed tiny blooms only inches from the earth for many months. I set the aperture and, with a little of Betty's reflected light, snapped the picture.

Then her sharp eyes spotted another group of Trout Lilies. "Lord, Miz Greene, look at those over there. They're open, too."

"Oh, yes," I exclaimed as though we'd found the treasure at the end of a rainbow. I was thrilled to see so many bell-shaped blossoms which were a delicate shade of yellow, perfect for the photograph, but I realized I'd have to shoot them barely an inch above the ground. The wind felt colder and it was turning dark. I didn't think I'd have enough light, even with the reflector. Since I didn't really want to take a flash shot, I decided to give up on the Trout Lilies for that day. Besides, it was getting too cold for Betty. "Let's take a chance that the freeze will leave a few Trout Lilies. We can come back next week," I said.

"Good, I'm about to freeze to death!" she said. As we hurried along the trail toward the car, Betty's story of Loretta joining the army drifted back into my mind.

"What happened between you and Loretta?" I asked her.

"Well, before we went over to Montgomery, I thought Loretta was gonna' stay in school," Betty continued with her story. "She was gonna' be an accountant."

"What did you do?" I asked.

"I got real mad when I thought she was leaving school to join the army. But, after she explained that she wasn't really leaving college, I calmed down. I found out she'll be able to stay in college. It'll just take her a year longer to graduate."

"If that's true, then why did she do it?" I asked.

"This way her tuition is paid for, and she'll have a good job when she finishes school." Betty smiled as she said, "So now I'm glad she did it... but I was sure shocked when she first told me. It was the last thing I was expectin'."

"Well, if I'd stayed on my planned course this morning photographing only lilies, the day would have been wasted. I would have missed the Anemones, and they really gave me a gladness of heart. They were so pretty and delicate. Oftentimes, we're like that, so intent on one goal or course that we fail to see other opportunities around us. Sometimes all it takes to make one happy is to open the heart and be willing to take a second look."

We drove back out through the gardens passing early blooming Flame Azaleas along the way. "You know you're right, Miz Greene," Betty said after a few minutes. "It seems like when we open our hearts lookin' for the good in something, that's when God shows us something else good in a way we're not expectin' ... like you seeing those Anemones instead of the lilies, and me finding good in Loretta's joining the army. I guess, sometimes, God jus' likes to give us surprises!"

"Yeah, Betty," I laughed. "And, today His surprise came through a patch of wildflowers."

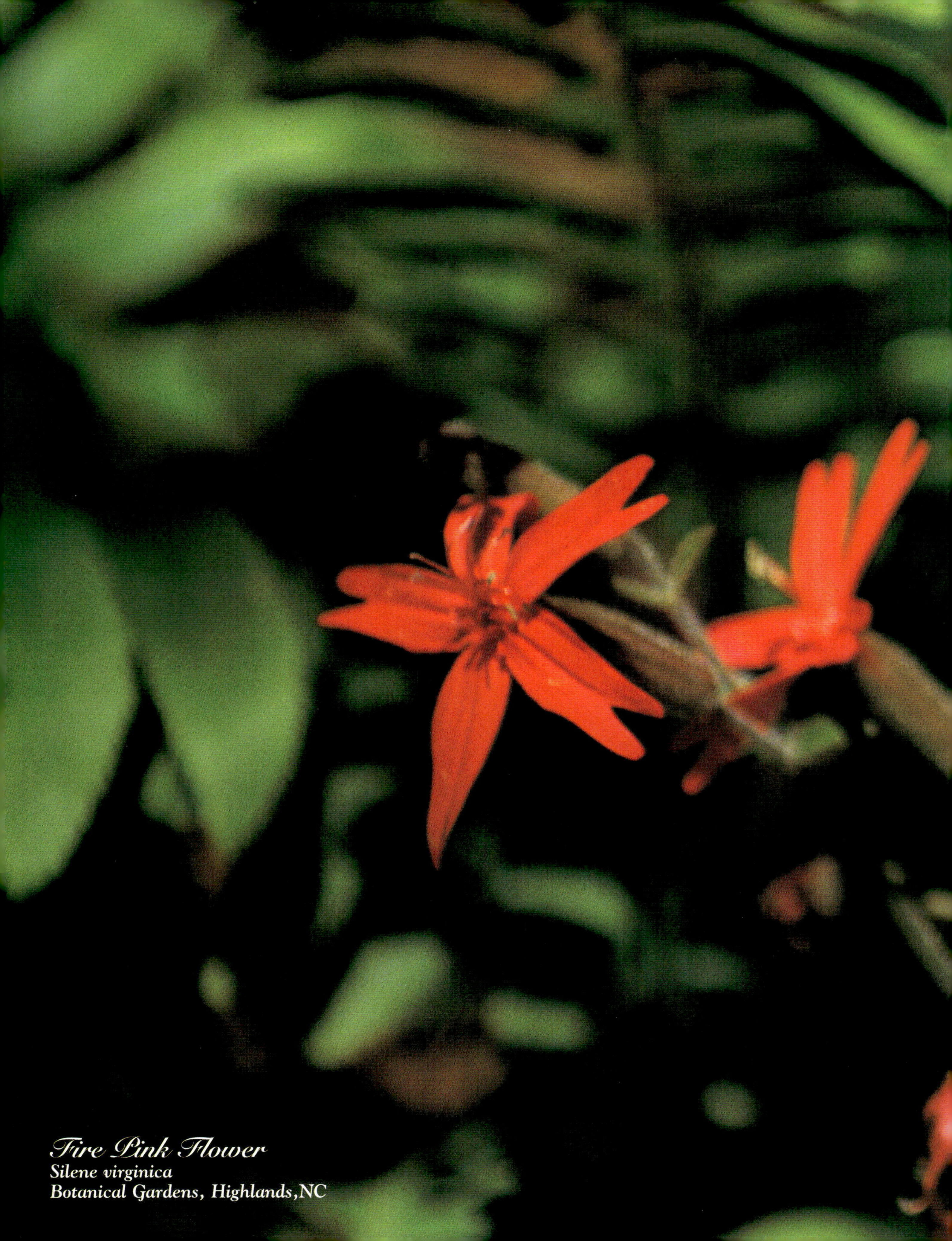

Fire Pink Flower
Silene virginica
Botanical Gardens, Highlands, NC

Wildflower Ritual

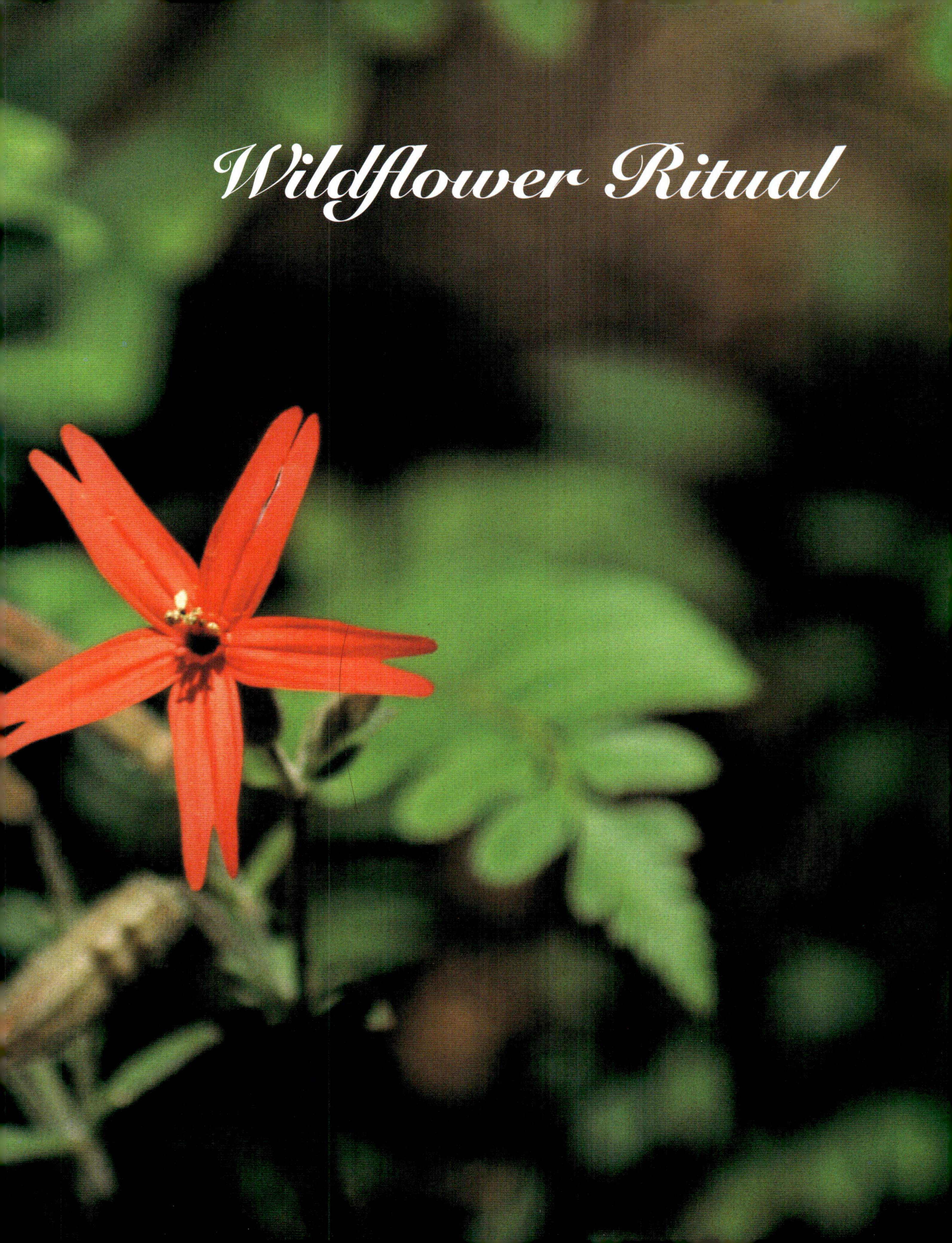

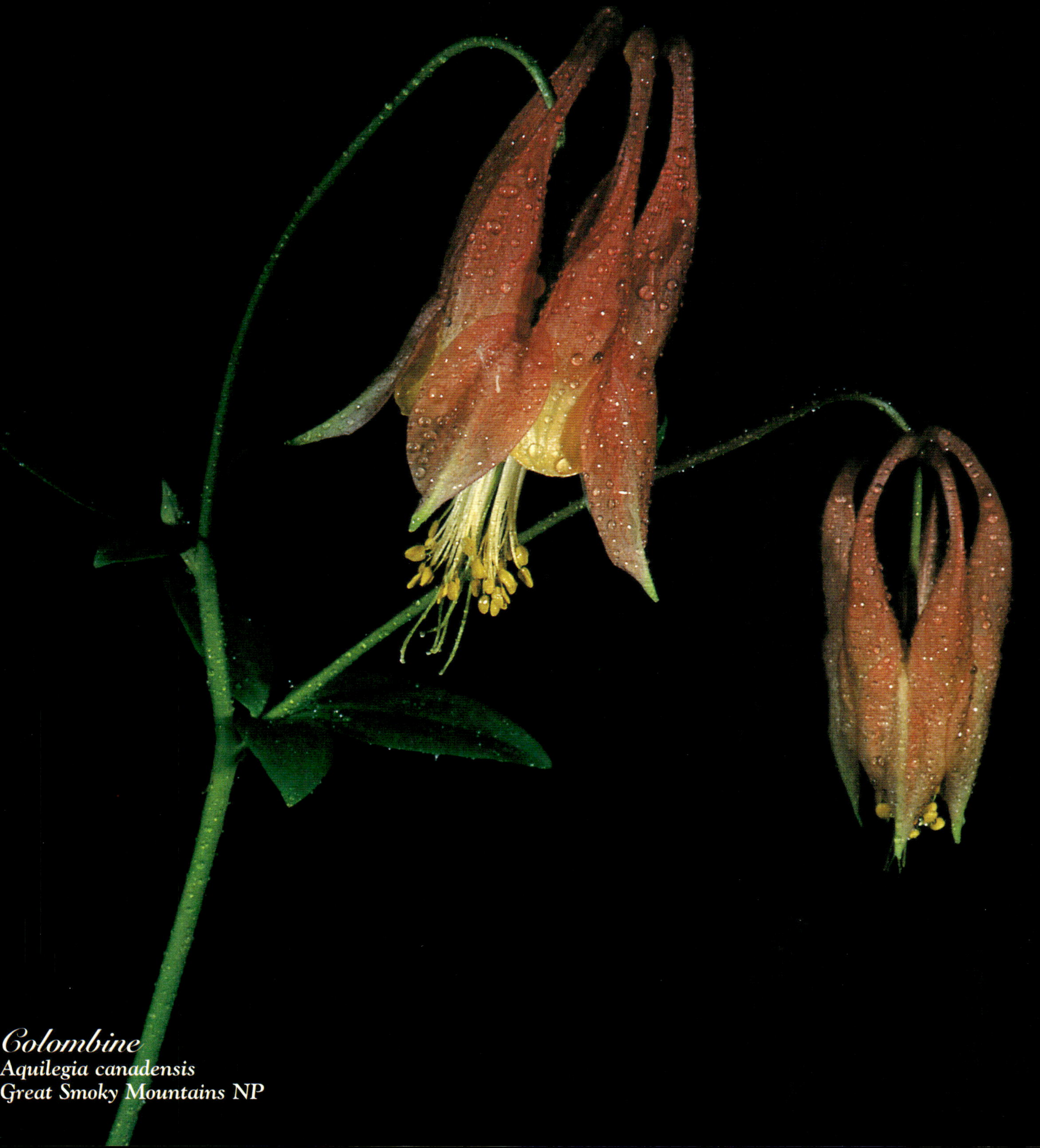

Colombine
Aquilegia canadensis
Great Smoky Mountains NP

Wildflower Ritual

"Brief beauty of the Columbine
heartens April morn.
It bursts its soul in pink and gold
flighting moments to adorn."
Angela Burns

My friend, Sister Josepha, a nun from Holy Trinity, Alabama, was having lunch with me one day when she said, "Janie, every Tuesday night a group meets at the retreat house for focusing sessions. Why don't you come? There's power in group focusing."

"If anyone needs guidance on focusing, I'm the best candidate," I said laughing. At a Yale workshop, she'd learned to teach people to focus their lives, and I thought it would be helpful to have some directed experience in focusing. I could still remember even in my high school annual the editors wrote that I was scattered. Still at 64, I'd find myself involved in too many projects, not really focused on any one of them. This habit of spreading myself thin was draining my energy.

With a twinkle in her eyes Sister Josepha said, "You certainly stayed focused long enough to finish your book *Dancing Feathers*."

"Yes," I said, "finishing is not my problem, but I have such a long list of interests that staying focused and making the choice of what I should focus on is a problem."

Although I really wanted to go, I declined Sister's invitation because we were already into Spring, and, like everyone else, I had an accelerated schedule in April. As usual, I was busy with too many projects. It was as if life had a lasso around my neck, jerking me here and there, and I had no power or control. I'd wanted to honor my Wildflower Ritual month, but how was I to get away from all my commitments?

Then one night I read in one of Alexander Stoddard's books, "Choice is the rudder that guides each person's destiny." Those words made me realize I was allowing many of my choices to be directed by the flow of other people's lives, acting from without instead of from within. I needed to make time for my own commitments, to focus and be true to my inner self. So, for my April 5th birthday, I gave myself permission to go to the Blue Ridge Mountains in North Carolina to photograph wildflowers.

As I approached Highlands, I saw a meadow filled with Bluets and felt a new energy as I thought about photographing the lilac carpet of wildflowers. I stopped the car and walked quietly through the morning fog toward the meadow. I could hear water splashing from the spillway of a small pond at the entrance of the field. The song birds were flying about feeding on the new mown grass, each singing his own song. The air still felt winter-cold. My sneakers were so wet with dew my feet were freezing. Suddenly, I heard a loud splash, and saw a beaver making a wide wake as he swam for his life trying to escape from me....an intruder into his sacred space. The tall Hemlocks shaded the tiny Bluets which were bent from heavy dew. I felt like Thoreau when he wrote "Heaven is under our feet as well as over our heads." Here was a peace I hadn't known in a long, long time; moreover, clarity of thought was mine. The scene was so full of nature's abundance; I wondered why I'd procrastinated so long in honoring my vow to be with the wildflowers in April. Why hadn't I come to the mountains sooner? It was as though, once I'd entered the different environment, I began to focus more clearly.

The light was still too low to get any good photographs, so I drove over to the Botanical Gardens where Bill, the grounds-keeper and resident wild flower expert, was standing in front of the building gathering fallen limbs. His list of wildflowers in bloom is published each week in the Highlands Newspaper. Bill knows wildflowers like a journalist knows words.

"Good morning, Bill," I said, thankful that he was there to direct me to the blooming Lady's-slippers.

"I'm sorry," he said, "you're too early for the Lady's-slipper. They're not blooming yet."

"Ohhh, no," I groaned, "that means another trip." But he directed me to flowers I could photograph, blooming Trillium, yellow and purple violets, Columbine, Jack-in-the-Pulpit. "I give lectures about the medicinal value of plants," he said.

"What is it about the wildflowers that you like so much?" I asked Bill.

"Well," he said, "my daddy didn't finish beyond the third grade, but he knows all about wildflowers, and their medicinal value better than anybody I know...and I guess you might say I was raised on wildflowers."

"But Bill, what in particular makes them so special to you?" I asked.

"Maybe it's because I believe God puts every one of them here. The smaller they are, the prettier they are, and I guess I'm just glad to have the privilege of working in this part of God's beauty in nature."

He told me that the Lady's-slipper wouldn't be blooming for a couple of weeks, and since he was having knee surgery to replace some cartilage, he wouldn't be there when they bloomed.

"Do you really think you'll feel like coming back to work in two weeks?" I asked the tall lanky man, hardly believing he could do his work there in the gardens so soon after surgery.

"Oh, yes," he said, "they told me it would be only two weeks. I don't like to have anyone else help in the gardens," he continued. "As much as they help, they don't always know the wildflowers, and sometimes they dig 'em up."

I told him how frustrating it had been wanting to come to North Carolina and yet unable to get away until now. "I've been so busy," I told him. "I really wanted to get up here and photograph all the wildflowers in season, but I haven't had time."

"You're like the story I heard about the man who said, 'I stay so busy I can't get a thing done!'" he laughed.

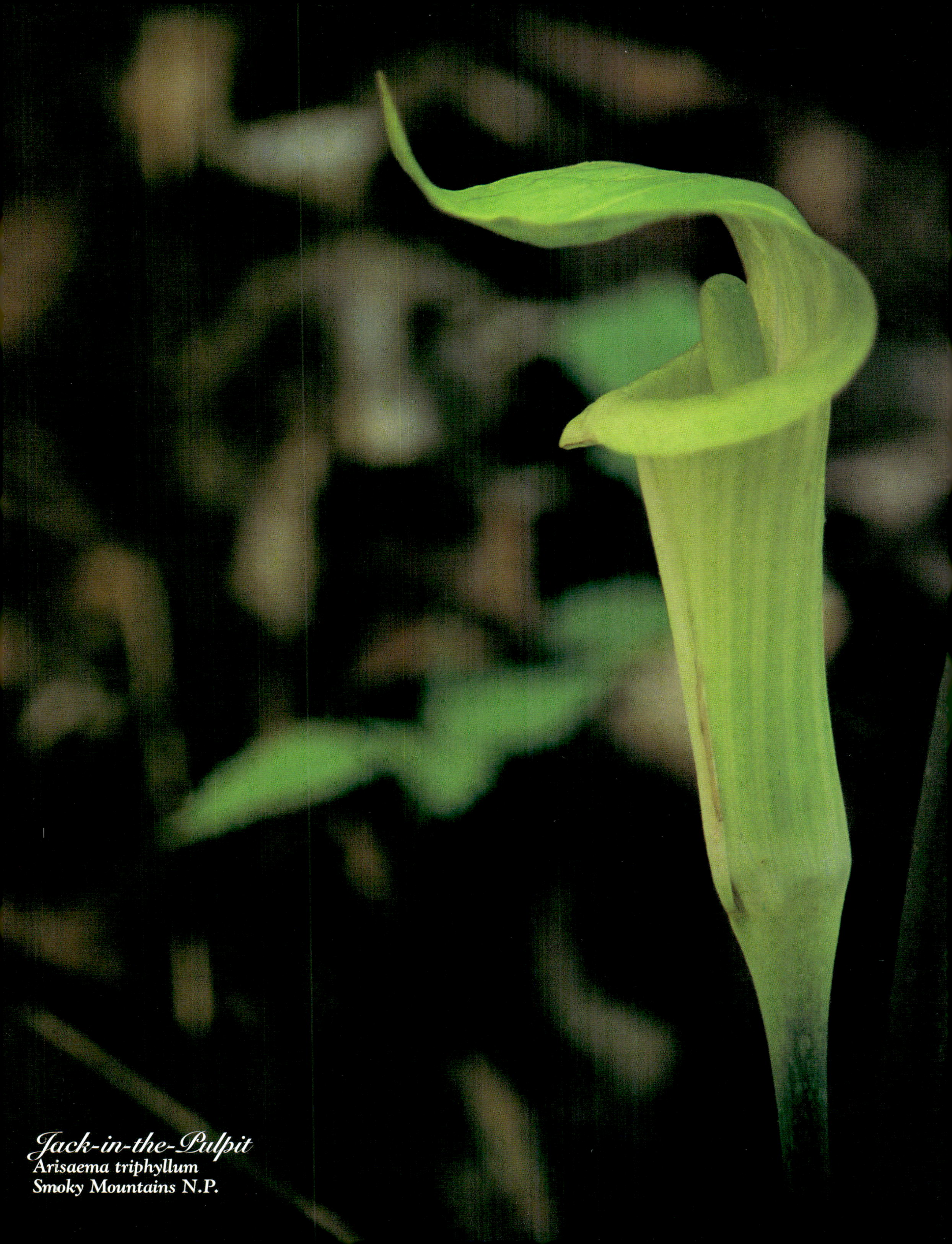

Jack-in-the-Pulpit
Arisaema triphyllum
Smoky Mountains N.P.

With my tripod on my shoulder and cameras around my neck, I followed Bill to a lovely group of Trilliums. I was huffing and puffing, but the hills were nothing to him. We walked the entire garden trying to see what was there and blooming before I set up the tripod. Once we found the area with the white Trillium, I stopped to set up the camera and Bill ambled on while wishing me good luck with the photography.

I grabbed one end of the tripod, then another and another, until I had extended the poles the length I thought they needed to be. Then I clicked the legs so they'd straddle like a spider sitting in the sand. But that position didn't fit the slant of the earth. I sat down in the dirt beside the blossoms on the steep incline. Once I felt confident that the tripod would work, I slipped my camera into the quick-release and screwed the plate tight. Switching it on, I adjusted the depth of field to F22 and looked through the viewfinder only to find that the red battery light was flashing. "Dang," I muttered under my cold breath, "I guess the cold ruined my battery." Losing all my inspiration, I reached into my jacket pocket, found a new battery, and tried one more time to get down low enough to see the flower in the viewfinder. Then, somehow I pushed the camera off the center and had to re-adjust and tighten the screw so it wouldn't slip again.

I sat there for a moment trying to compose myself and looked at the camera and sprawling tripod. That's me, I thought, twisted here and turned there. I'd felt so unfocused as I tried to escape all the frustration and confusion of trying to do too much. Why hadn't I gone to Sister Josepha's focusing sessions, I wondered. Of course I'd wanted to photograph the wild Lady's-slipper, and if I were going to see any, I had to get up here in April. Plus, if I wanted to honor my April wildflower ritual, I knew it was necessary to get into the mountains before the trees put out their leaves and spread a canopy over the carpet of colorful Spring flowers.

But it was just as confusing there trying to make the camera and tripod work to photograph flowers as it was at home trying to get all my household projects done. There's really no escape, I realized. Anything we do that is worthwhile takes energy, patience, and skill. We have to learn to focus on what is important and to deal with whatever confusion is involved. Maybe my life was not any more complicated than anyone else's. Wasn't Bill going to have to stop work in this gorgeous natural environment and have knee surgery? Things were not running smoothly for him either.

I thought of the advice my friend Sue Monk Kidd gave on one of her reasons for stumbling on the creative path: "It is often a lack of focus, allowing my energy to run out in dozens of directions," she wrote, " many of them silly tributaries of distraction rather than setting priorities and funneling my energy toward the project at hand." She went on, "It's true that power can come from the flexibility of doing many things, but sometimes the multiplicity, the moving from one thing to another, is overdone and we diffuse our power. There are times it is best to dam up the tributaries and send the energy thundering in just one direction."

It seemed that my energy was moving in hundreds of tributaries. And I didn't have an ounce of power to even photograph one wildflower. I had let circumstances frustrate me and cause my inner self to become as confused as the funny-looking tripod. Feeling discouraged, tired and unable to get all the work done, the beautiful peaceful scene from earlier that morning was forgotten. I was absorbed with the technicalities of the camera and tripod, going off in "silly tributaries." I'd forgotten my purpose in photographing the wildflowers...I was supposed to be honoring a ritual of being present to the beautiful flowers in April...remembering my mother's lessons there among the wildflowers. So I took a deep breath of the cool air and spent a few moments just enjoying the beauty around me, the quietness, the light falling through the branches of the trees. I'd remembered a man on television once saying that if a camera is focused, you can see clearly...provided the light is there." Perhaps that was all I'd needed...a little light on both the camera and my life at home.

When I finally turned back to the camera, everything seemed to go better. Soon, practically jumping from the camera lens, was the most beautiful Columbine I'd ever seen...an early Spring bloomer. The veins in the petals were clearly in focus. I was not even looking for Columbine flowers, but, here was my gift of the morning staring me in the face. It was lovely! I snapped the shutter quickly, satisfied that I had a perfectly focused picture.

I had been able to capture the beautiful pink and yellow bell-shaped bloom for my collection of wildflower photographs...because I had finally taken the time and trouble to put everything in the place it belonged...to focus properly. But I knew I had focused more than my camera that morning. I had managed to focus my life too... not at the retreat house, as Sister Josepha had suggested, although that would have been good, but even better still, I'd cast myself upon nature's breast, and found my lesson in her! I would remember the technicalities each time I turned on my camera, but I'd remember, too, the lessons I had learned there in the Botanical Gardens: to focus my life as well as the lens of my camera.

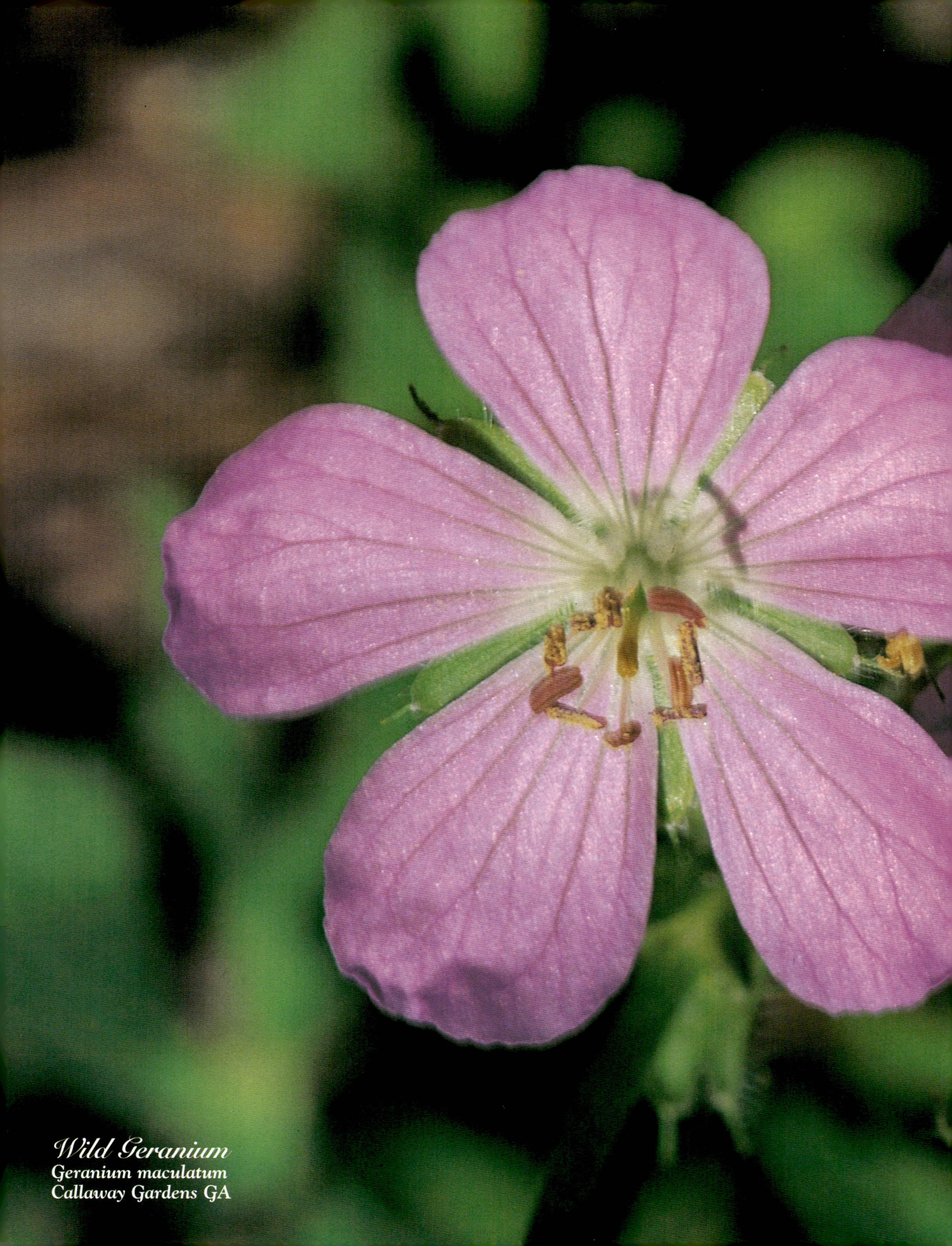

Wild Geranium
Geranium maculatum
Callaway Gardens GA

Hidden Blooms

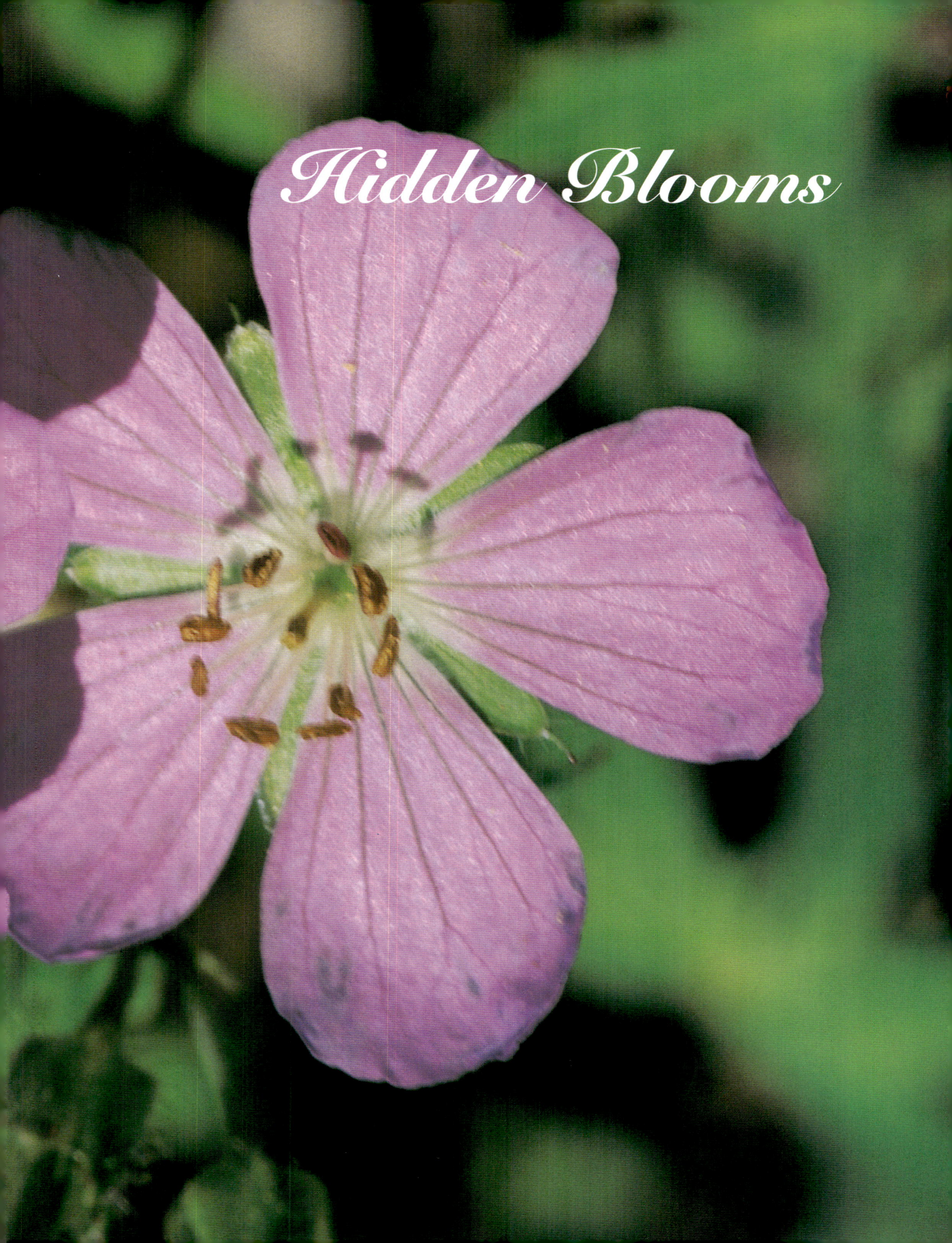

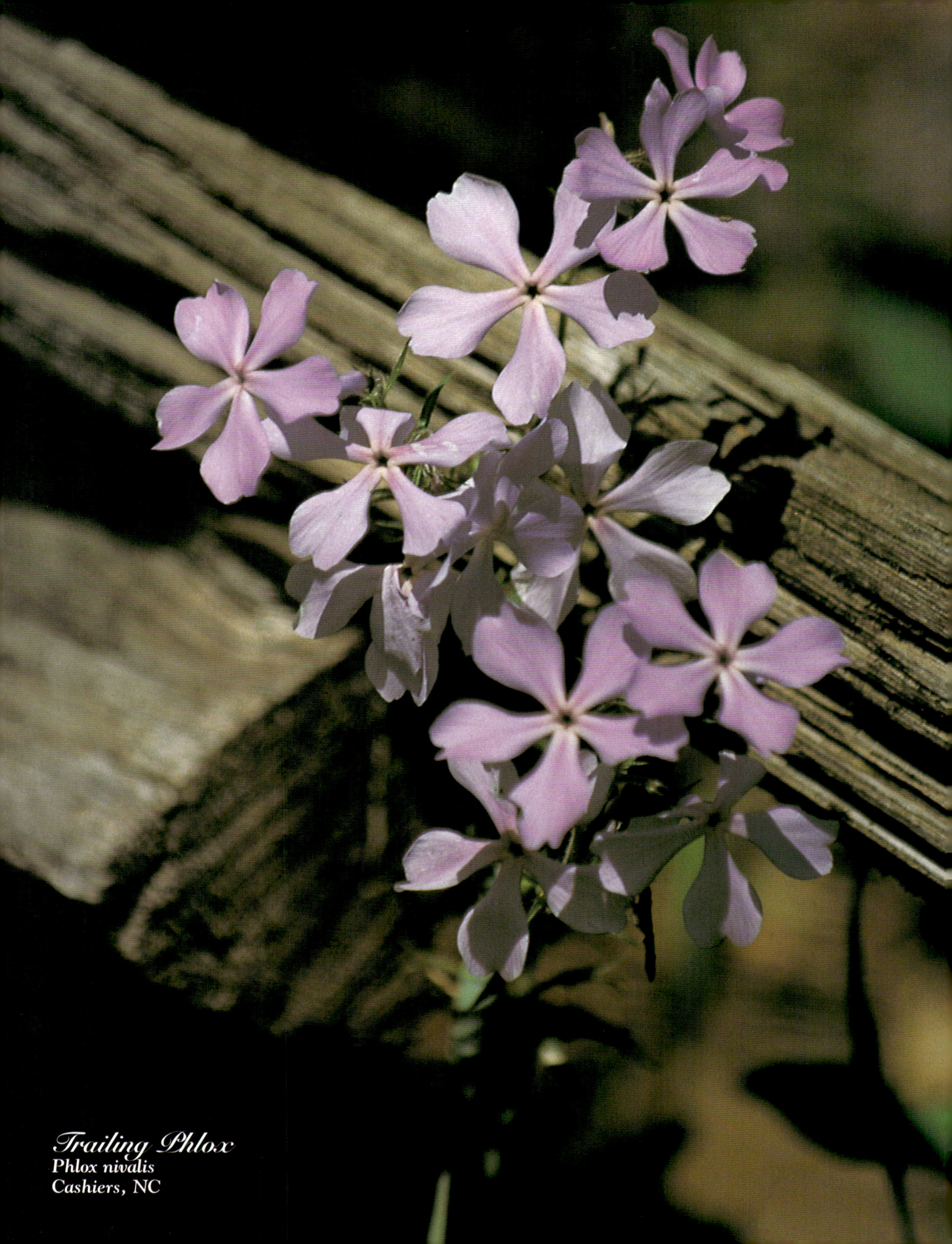

Trailing Phlox
Phlox nivalis
Cashiers, NC

Hidden Blooms

Show me the hidden things,
Take me down to the spring of my life,
and tell me my nature and my name.
Give me freedom to grow so that I may become
my true self - the fulfillment of the seed
which You planted in me at my making.
Out of the deep I cry unto thee, O God. Amen.

George Appleton

Like sunshine, my photograph of a yellow Lady's-slipper warmed me on an unusually cool day as I sat editing slides on the light table at home. Most of the time, editing was a chore I dreaded, but the orchid-like bloom in my transparency intensified my happiness that day. I'd just returned from the hospital where my namesake, Janie Lynne, had been born.

Sitting there in the sterile hospital room with the family gathered around our daughter-in-law Sandy's bed to welcome Janie Lynne into the world was such a happy time for everyone. As I looked at the blossom before me on my slide light table and remembered Janie Lynne's birth, I wondered what kind of bloom was hidden there inside that tiny baby the radiant mother was holding in the pink blanket. What was waiting to unfold? What would her life be like? What set of genes had she inherited? Who was she to become? What would her essence be? Would whatever was inside her remain true at twenty, forty or sixty years of age? Would she be able to find and know her hidden truth?

I picked up the yellow Lady's-slipper slide and filed it in the wildflower collection I'd been working on for a book idea. As I closed the drawer of the file cabinet, I remembered the day I was back in Highlands at the Botanical Gardens photographing the blooming Lady's-slipper.

I had gone to the entrance of the gardens and there, near the sign, I had seen a young college student working. "How is Bill?" I asked, remembering his knee surgery.

"He's getting along well after his surgery," he said. "In fact, he's scheduled to be back here today."

"This is my second trip to Highlands to photograph Lady's-slippers," I told him. "I was here three weeks ago, but they still weren't blooming."

"Well, you're in luck today," he replied, a youthful grin spreading across his face. "I saw one over here yesterday." Striding across the path, he led me to a tall Rhododendron bush and lifted its long limbs. I was thrilled to see the bright yellow wild orchid with its curled streamers hanging down on either side of the lily. I had finally found my Lady's-slipper to photograph!

The unfolding May leaves of the deciduous trees and the long narrow foliage of the Rhododendron bush created too much shade, so I ran back to the car to get my butterfly flash to make it possible to photograph in the dim light. I knew I wouldn't need a tripod, but I decided to use it anyway to better control the composition of the picture. As I fastened the flash and camera on a focusing rail and attached it to the tripod, I considered the Lady's-slipper and thought how glad I was that it was blooming now. But the beauty before me had not happened overnight. It seemed so sturdy and strong, but it had taken me two trips before I found it in bloom. The plant had to spend time rooting there in the dark, moist earth, beneath the snow and fallen leaves for a year, before it was ready to produce a blossom. It was necessary for it to have time to feed and grow before the green shoots finally began to reach toward the light.

It made me think of our own need as part of God's creation to be grounded before we bloom. It takes discipline, stillness, and being rooted in one place instead of running here and there the way I'd been doing for the last few weeks. Rooting for me meant maintaining loving relationships within my family and home. It also meant being creative with my nature photography and writing. Part of being rooted, too, meant knowing my limits as well as my strengths, and staying focused within my boundaries. Yes, I thought, if we are grounded in the proper environment, we can't help but bloom.

I wondered again what kind of bloom would my new granddaughter Janie Lynne, produce. I felt humbled that her mother had decided to give her my name, but even more than passing along my name, I hoped that I'd be able to give her the desire to come to know herself. I wanted to help her during those days and months and years as the bloom inside her developed. It wouldn't happen over night. It would take time. As the Greek writer Epictetus once wrote, "Nothing great is created suddenly, any more than a bunch of grapes or a fig. If you tell me that you desire a fig I answer you that there must be time. Let it first blossom then bear fruit and then ripen." Everything in nature takes time to sprout from a seed, grow, bloom and bear fruit. But, as surely as the golden Lady's-slipper hidden beneath the earth eventually emerges, the individual inside tiny Janie Lynne would develop into a radiant bloom which could touch others with its beauty. As her grandmother, I could help her by seeing that she was nurtured in the right soil and encouraging her to walk that sacred path and remain true to herself.

I wanted to remind her of her uniqueness. Among the billions of people living on earth, one of us may not be as talented or as graceful, as beautiful or as handsome as another, but each is unique. There is only one of each of us. Every individual has a certain set of genes and was born to do only the things that he or she can do. Mickey Rooney once said on a television program, "I learned early in life that I was the only one of me and I would make the best use of the only me there is." Robert Johnson wrote in his book, *Inner Work*, "to be our own selves, we stand on the surest ground."

Instead of trying to be like someone else or who someone else wants us to be, we need to learn to know ourselves completely and to develop our individual strengths

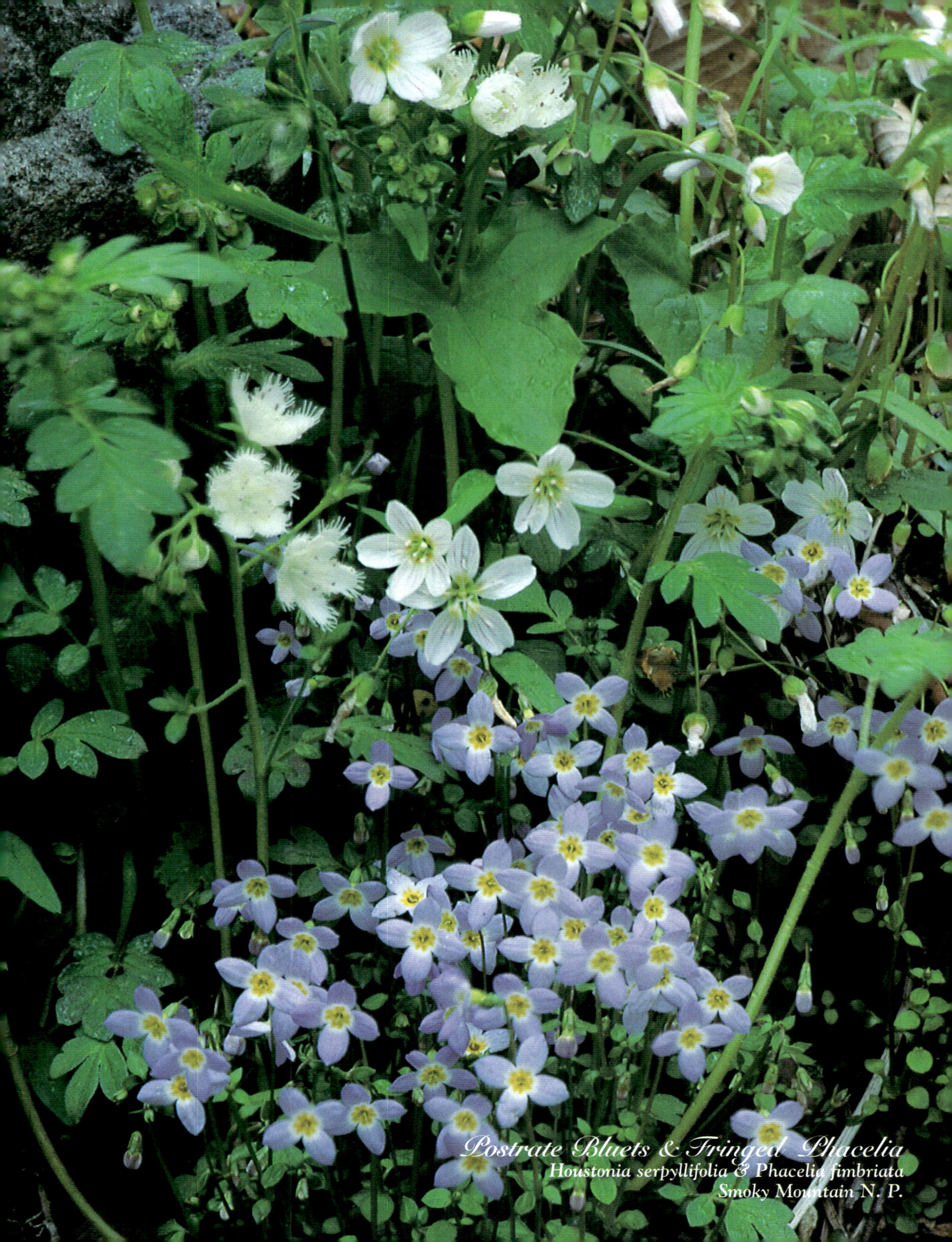

Postrate Bluets & Fringed Phacelia
Houstonia serpyllifolia & Phacelia fimbriata
Smoky Mountain N. P.

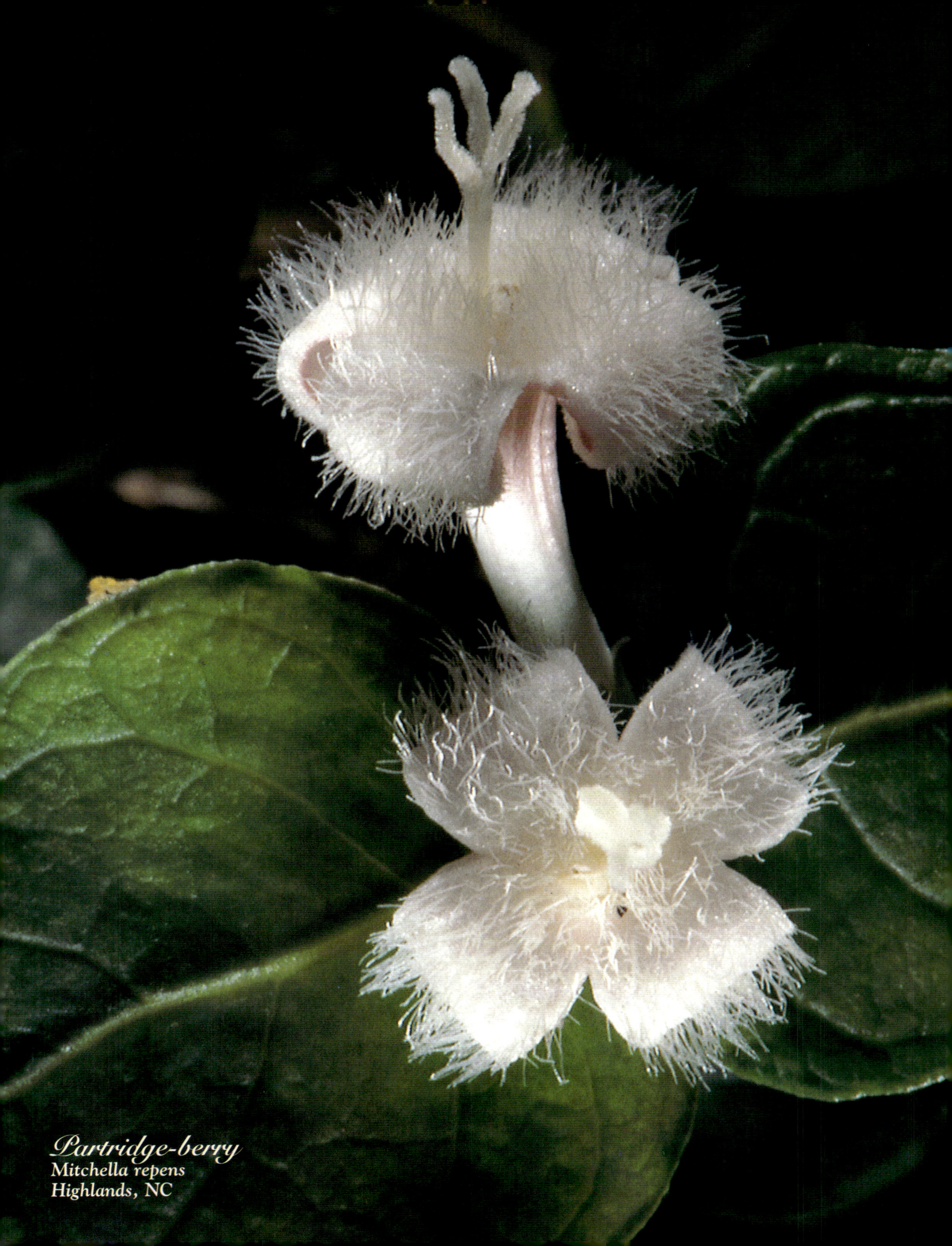

Partridge-berry
Mitchella repens
Highlands, NC

that are built into us. At Mama's church one day, I heard the minister say, "We hunger for acceptance and over-accommodate our lives for the world. We need to act from within, know who we are, accept ourselves just as God created us, and then stand on a strong foundation and act from the will of God within each of us." The Lady's-slipper didn't change because it grew beside the Rhododendron. It didn't try to be a Rhododendron. It remained true to what it was created to be. We need never feel less than, or rejected by another, if we remain true to ourselves. Of course we never like to be rejected by others. It isn't easy to feel rejected, but we can handle all the world's rejection if we don't reject ourselves and remain true to what God created us to be.

I looked up from the Yellow Lady's-slipper and saw Bill, the wildflower expert, walking up without the slightest limp. He was holding a cup of coffee and a book he'd been reading under his arm. "Hello Bill," I said, " I'm glad to see you're back in time to see the Lady's-slippers bloom. How'd your surgery go?"

"Everything went fine.... I'll be able to get back to work pretty soon," he said, still smiling as usual.

"I've met your assistant so it seems you'll have some good help for a while." As Bill turned to speak to another visitor walking by, I read the title of the book he was holding beneath his arm, *God Wants You To Be Rich*. I wondered why he was reading the book. Riches are already his, I thought, more than anyone could ever expect ...being there in the wildflower garden every day, meeting new friends, his mind and heart free to be the individual God created him to be.

As Bill continued to talk I reached over to touch the softness of the newborn flower. I hope our own newborn, Janie Lynne, will find Bill's kind of freedom, I thought, and learn to be happy walking her own sacred path. I knew it would not happen overnight. It would be a lifetime quest, but I hoped that she, like the Lady's-slipper developing inside the ground, would always accept her individuality and remain faithful to her unique blossom of truth.

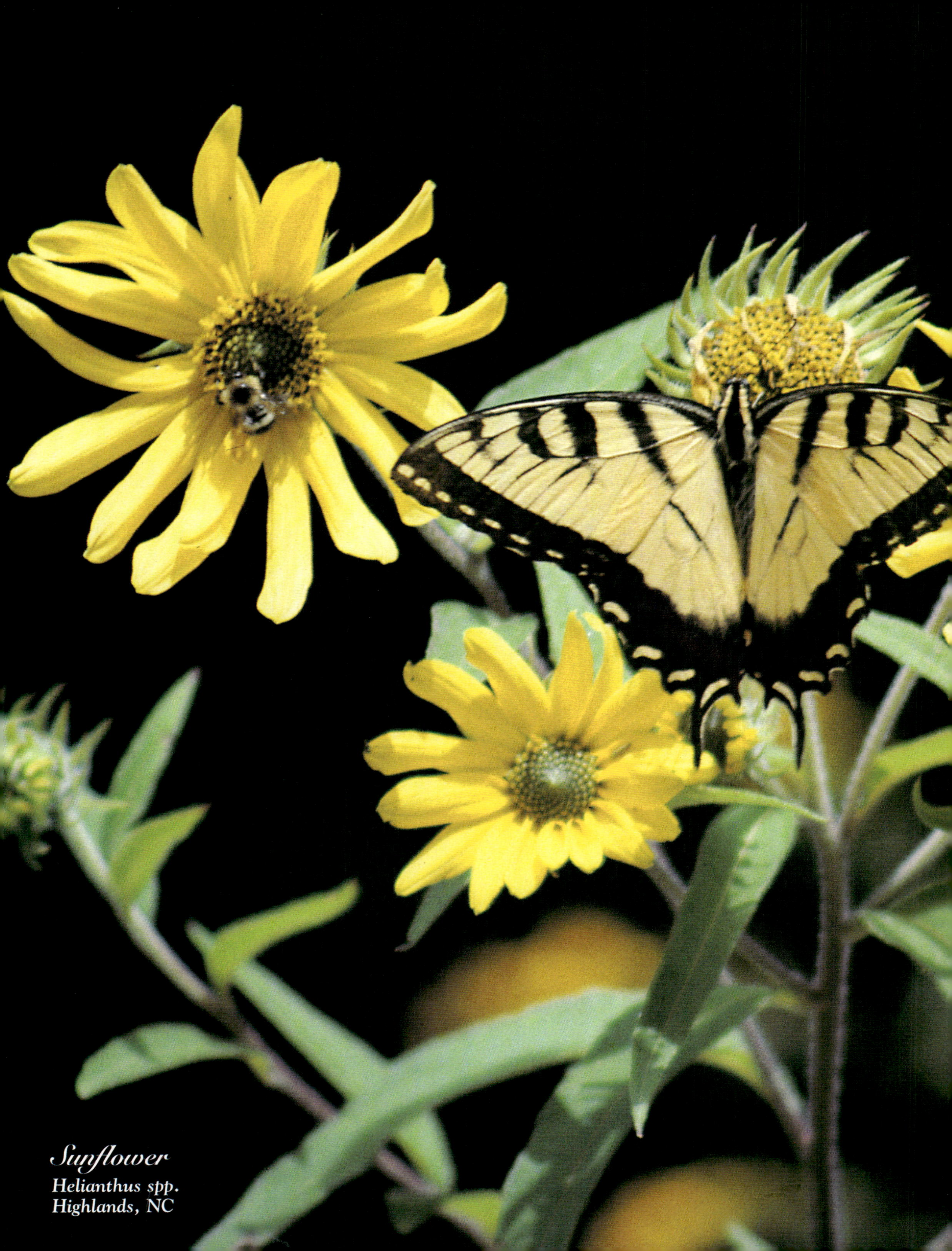

Sunflower
Helianthus spp.
Highlands, NC

Come join me now– use your imagination while we wander side by side through the wildflowers…

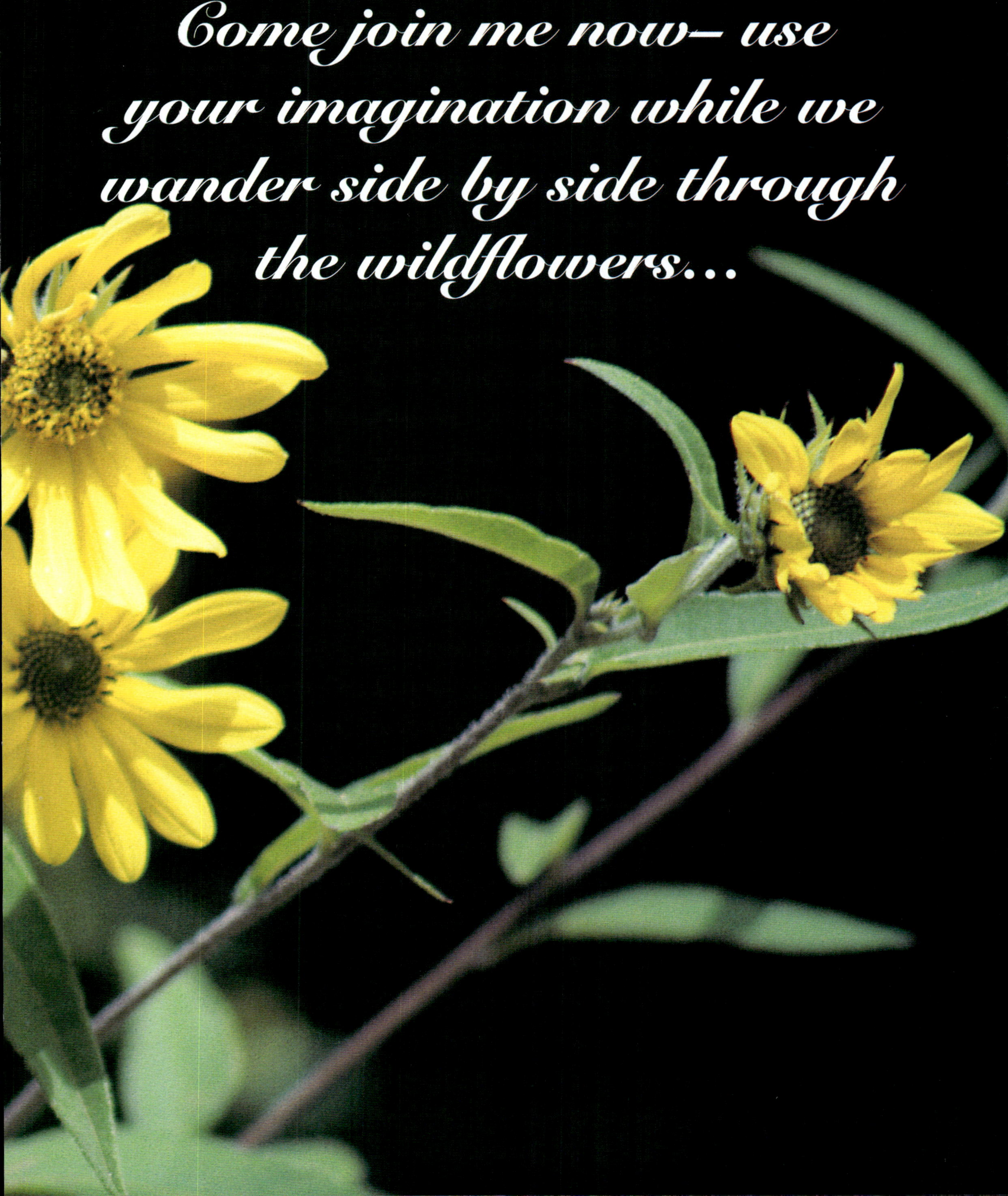

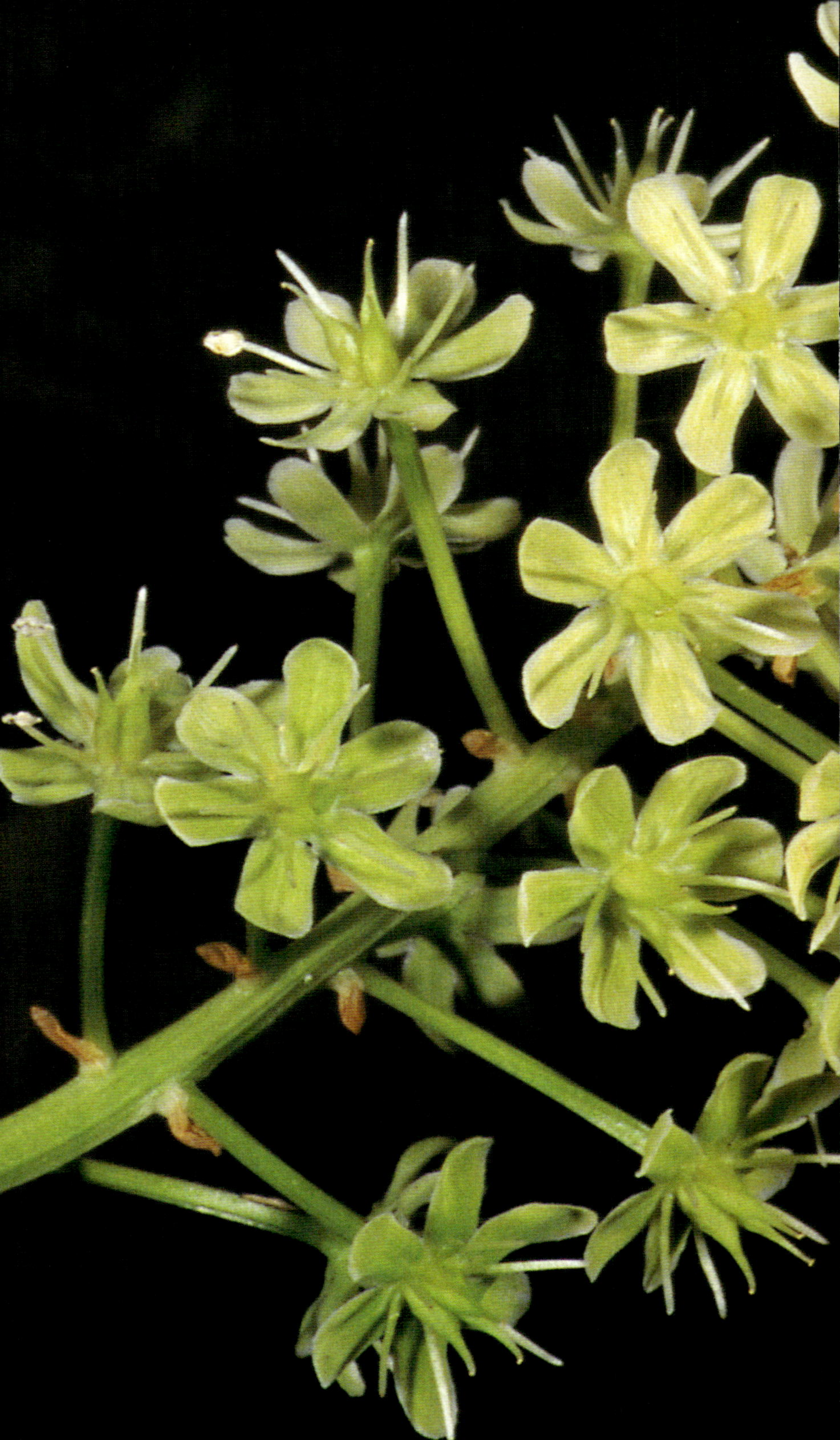

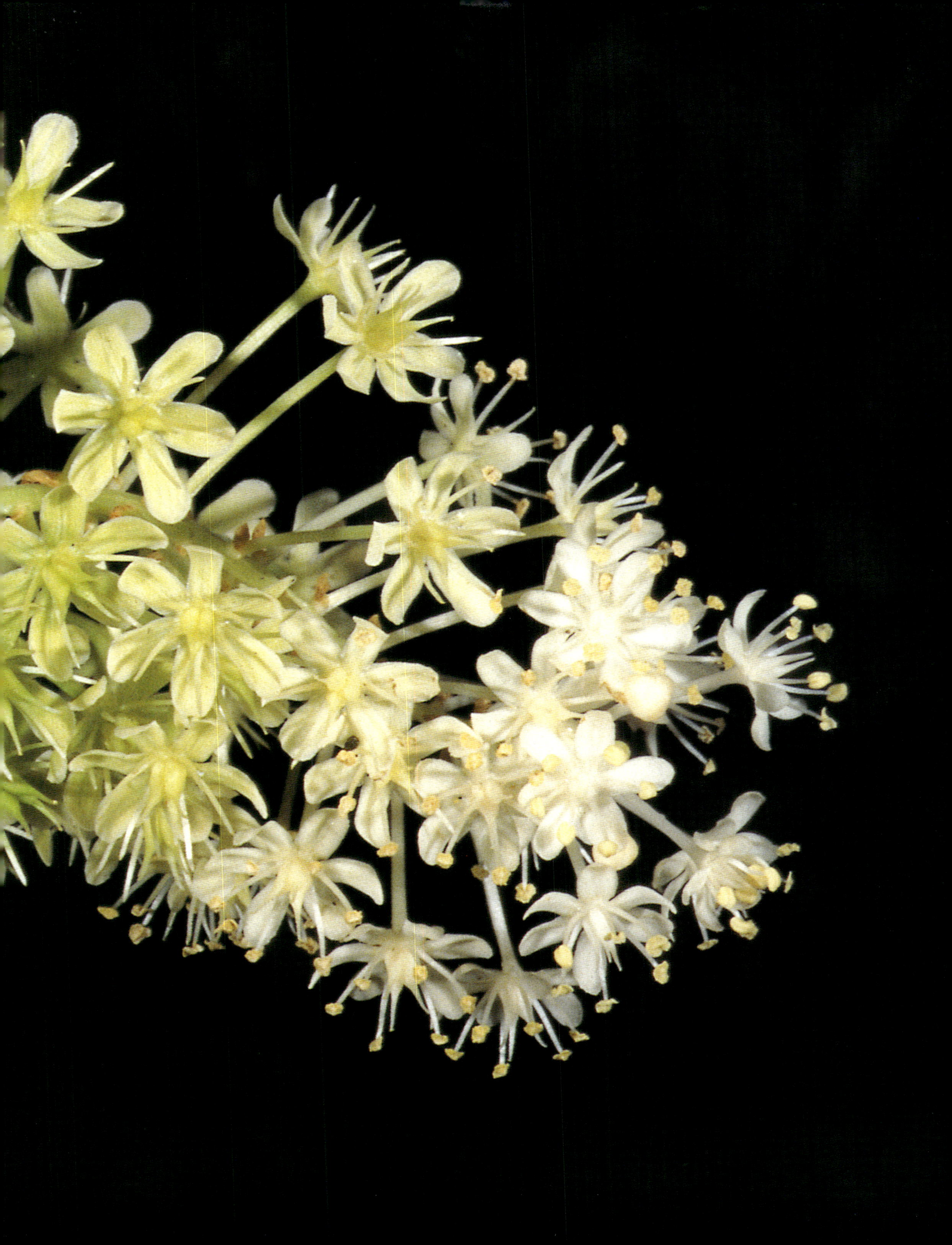

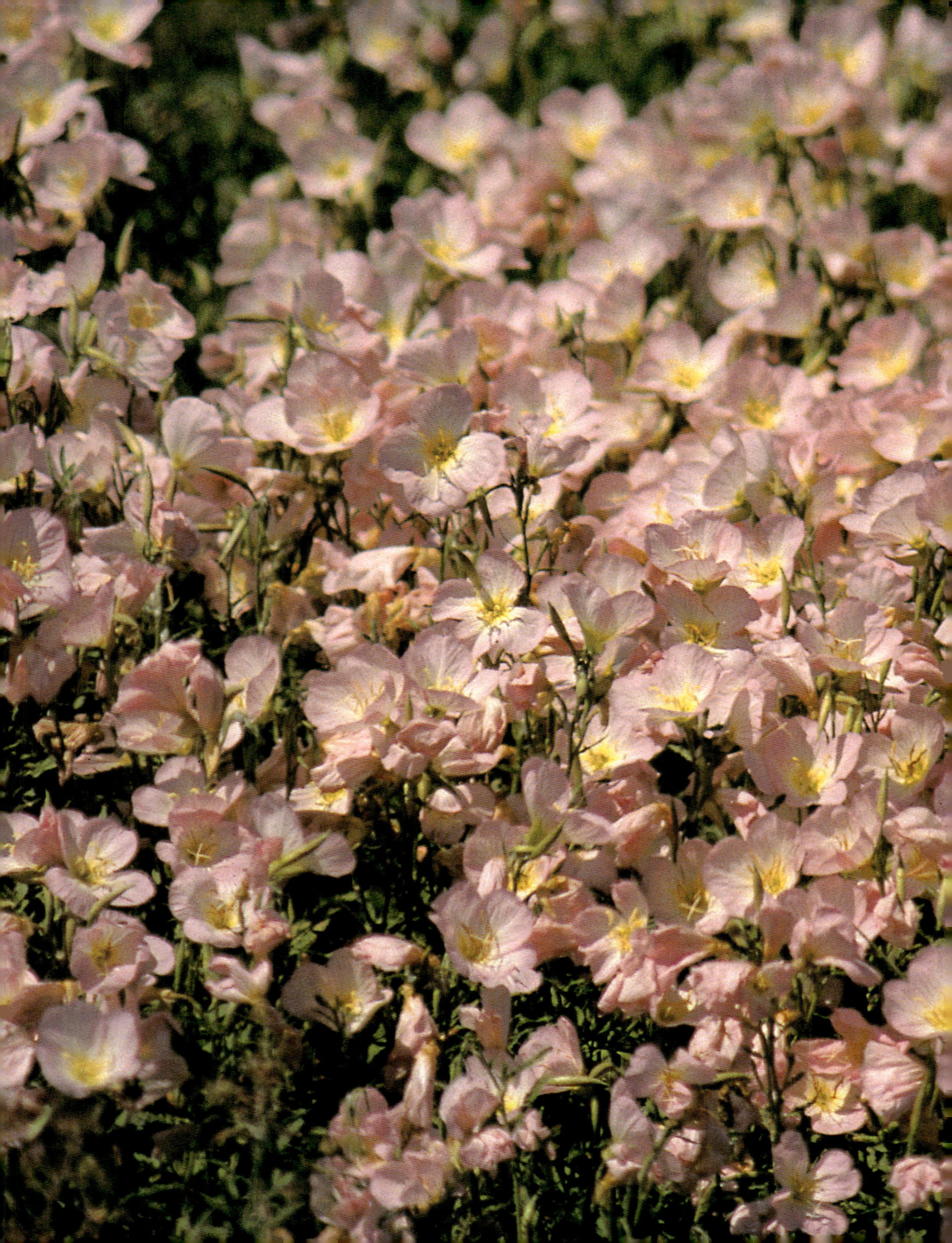

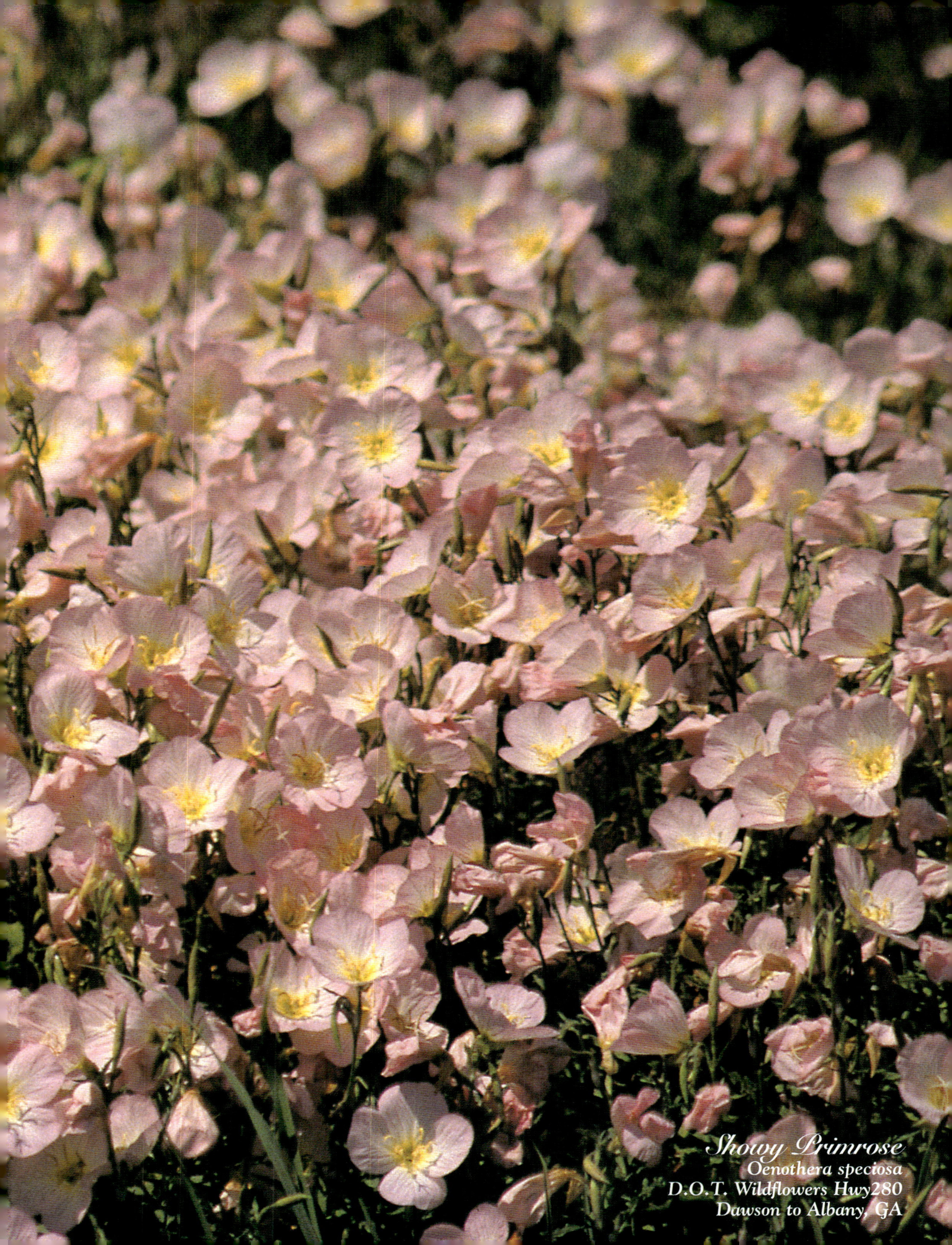

Showy Primrose
Oenothera speciosa
D.O.T. Wildflowers Hwy280
Dawson to Albany, GA

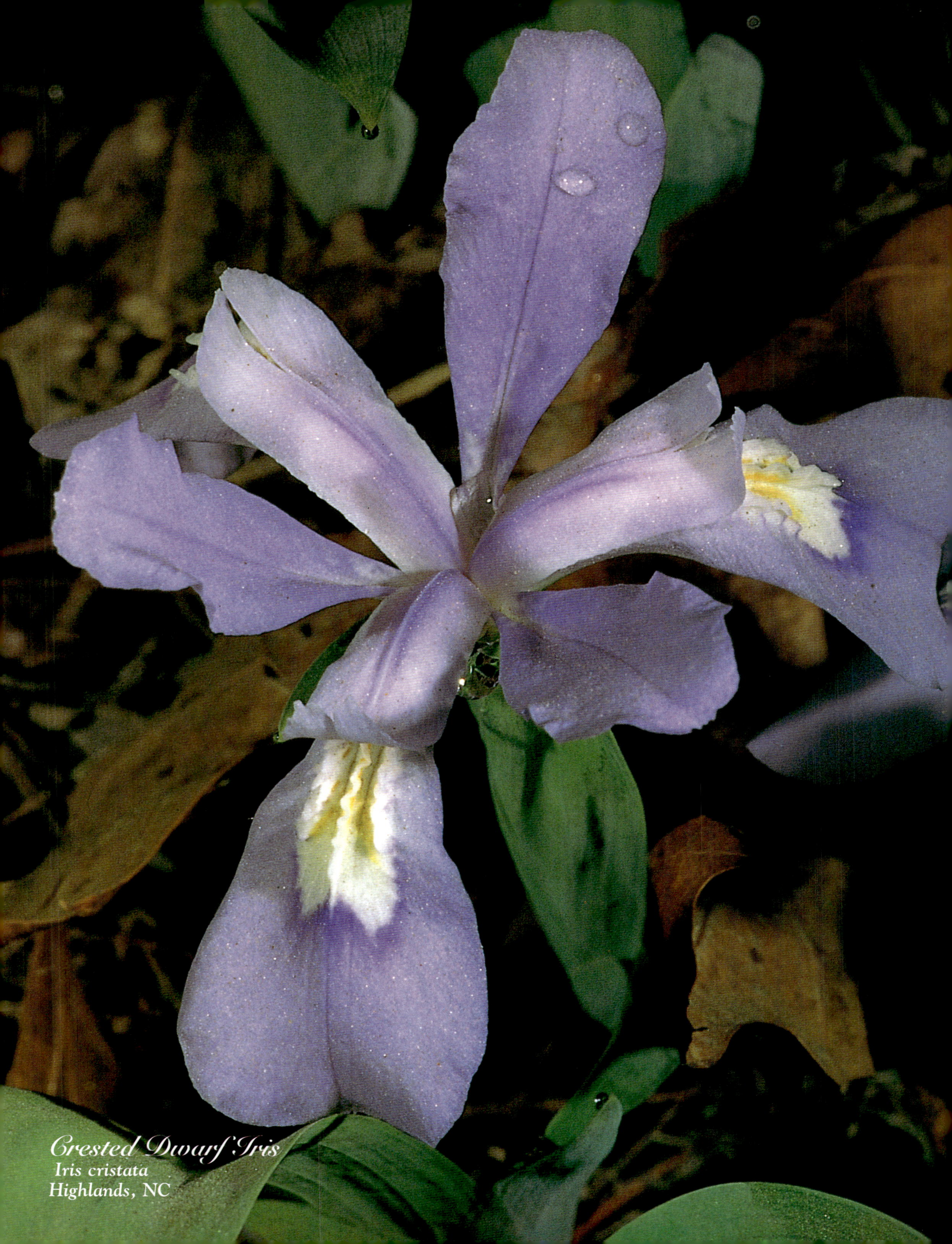

Crested Dwarf Iris
Iris cristata
Highlands, NC

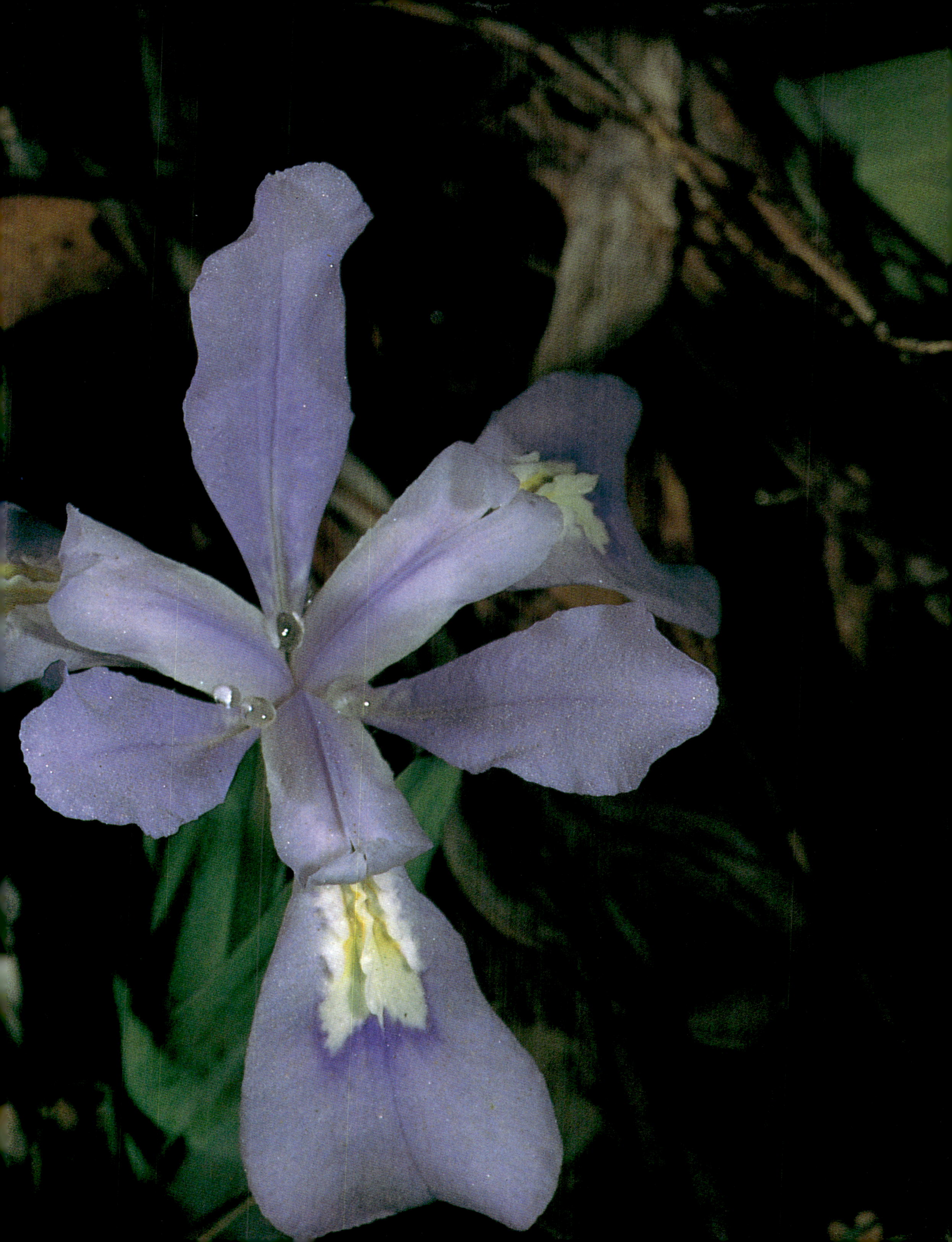

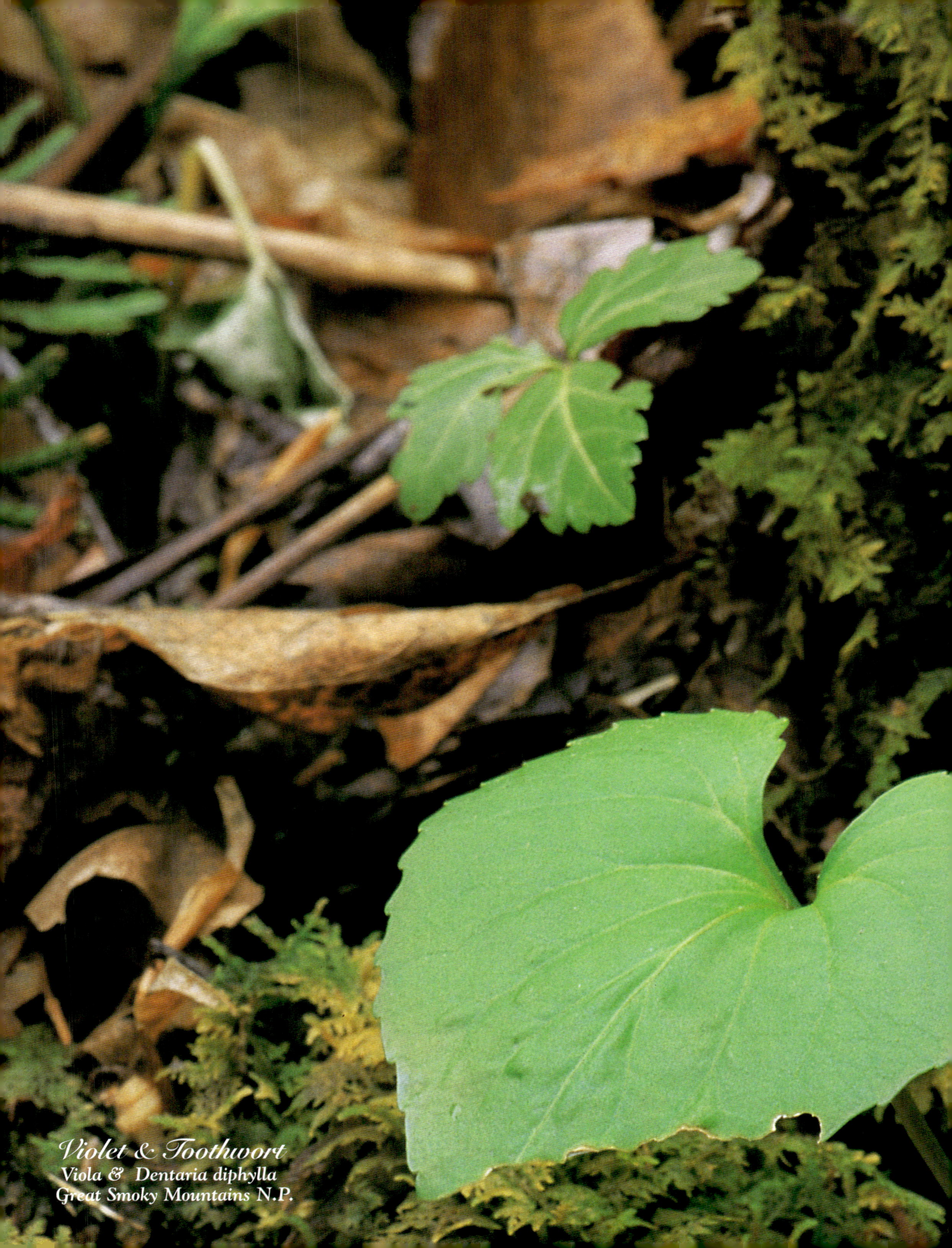

Violet & Toothwort
Viola & Dentaria diphylla
Great Smoky Mountains N.P.

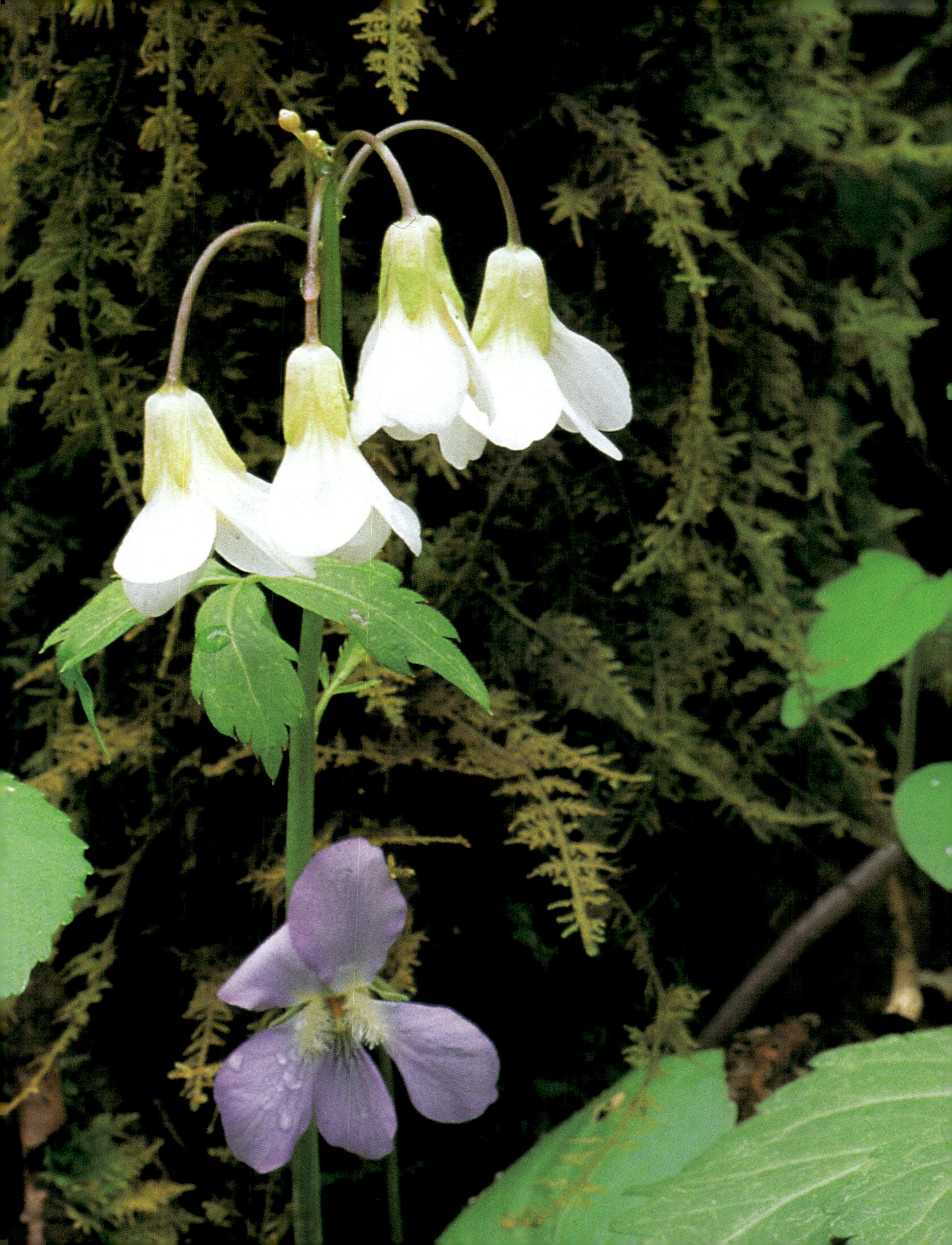

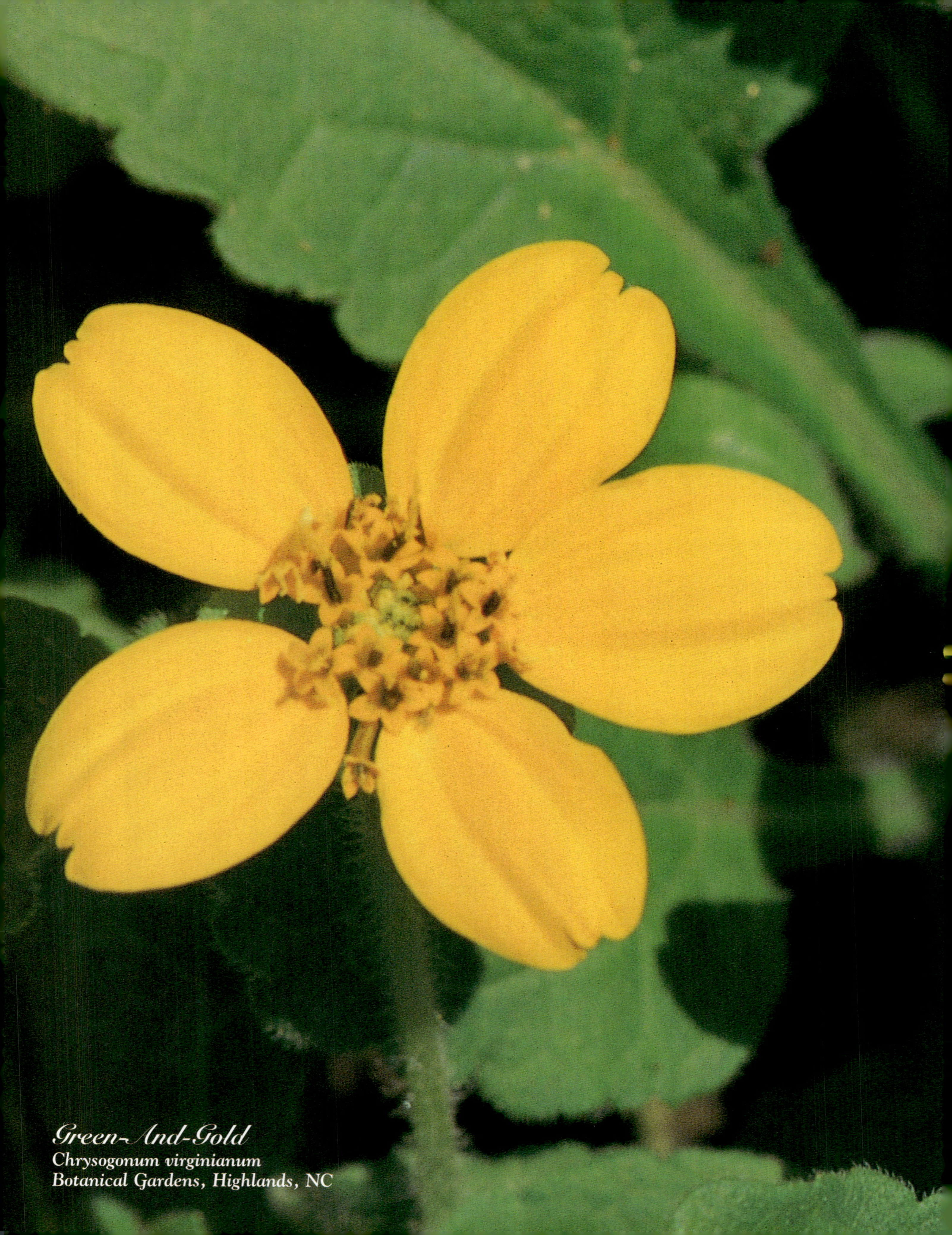
Green-And-Gold
Chrysogonum virginianum
Botanical Gardens, Highlands, NC

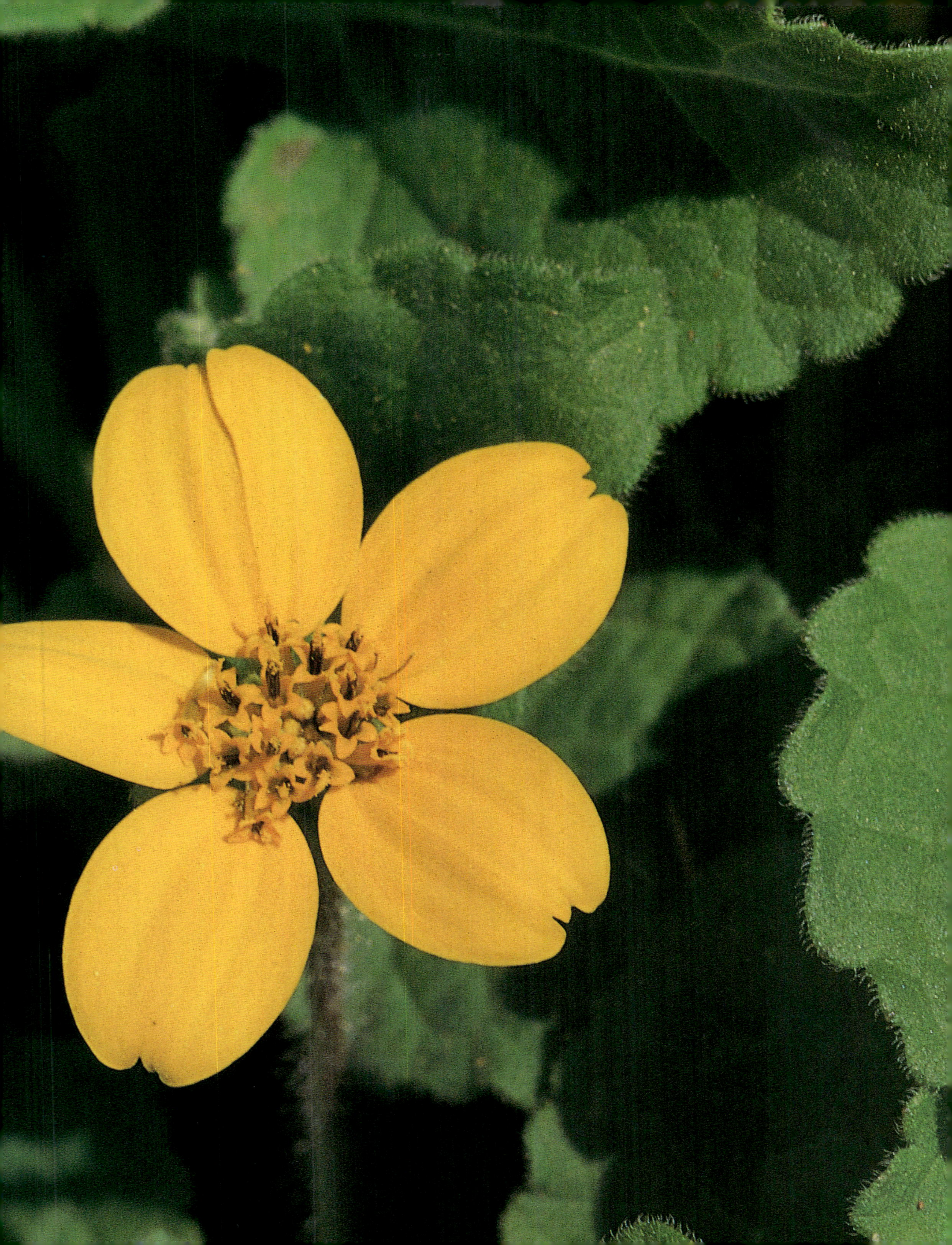

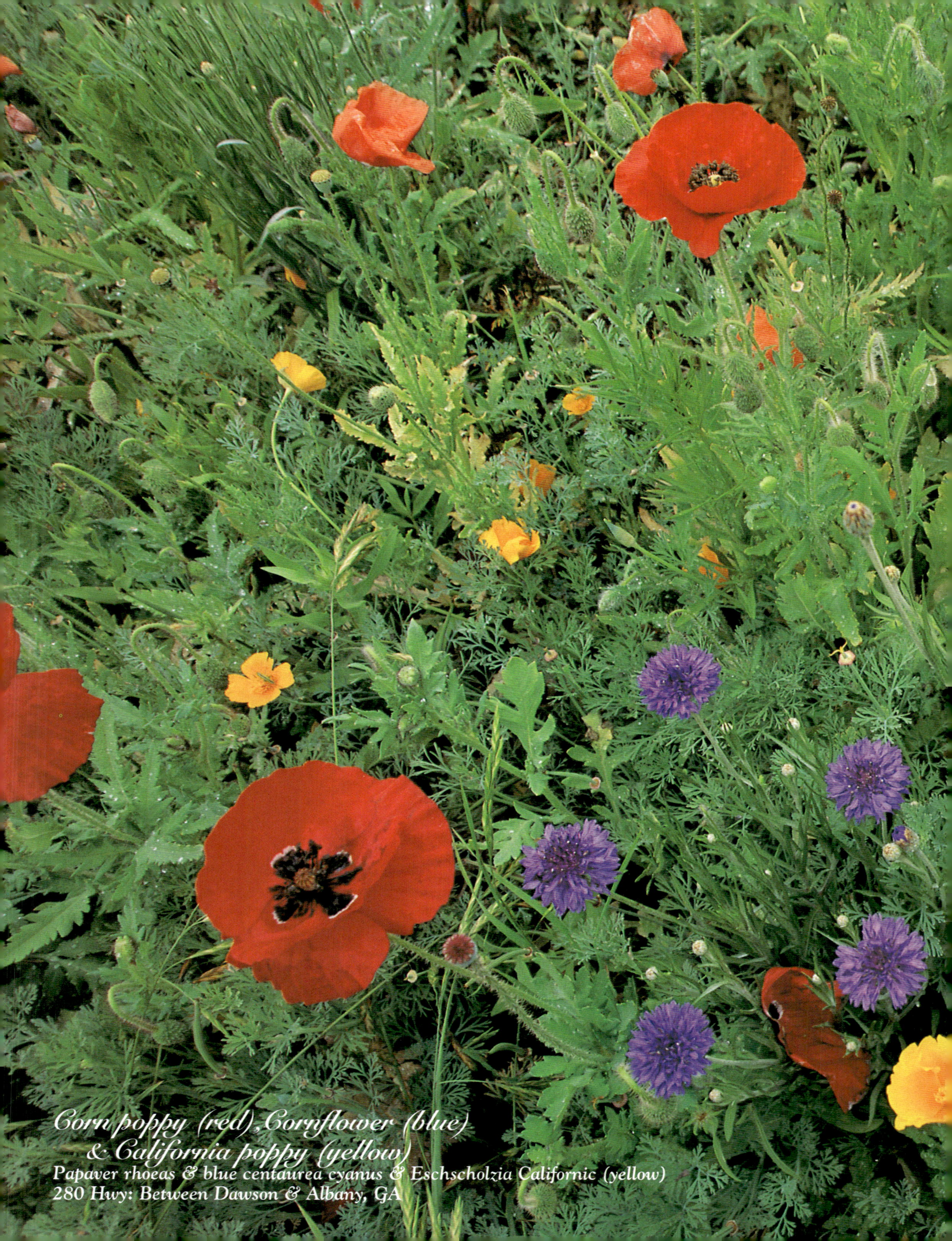

Corn poppy (red), Cornflower (blue) & California poppy (yellow)
Papaver rhoeas & blue centaurea cyanus & Eschscholzia Californic (yellow)
280 Hwy: Between Dawson & Albany, GA

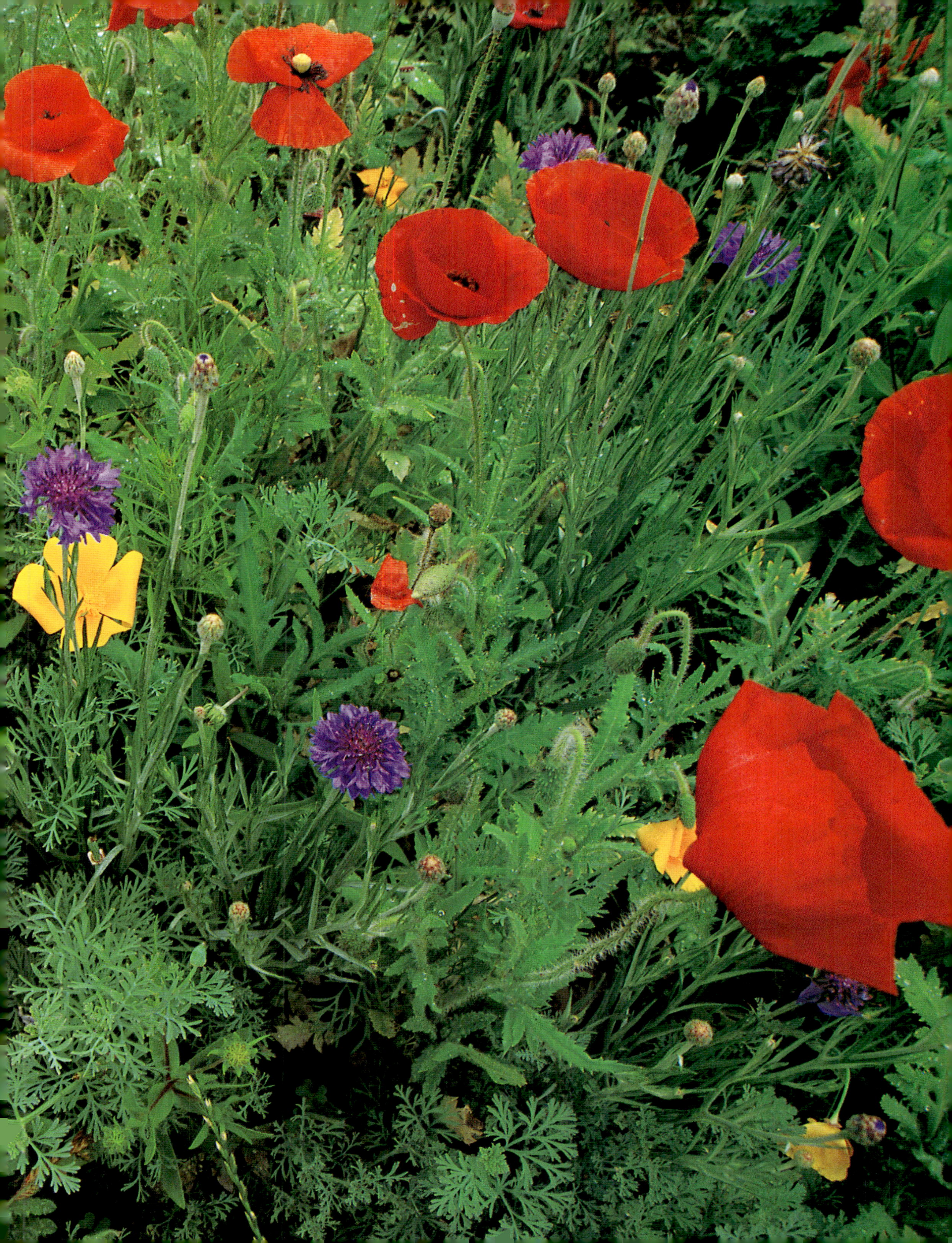

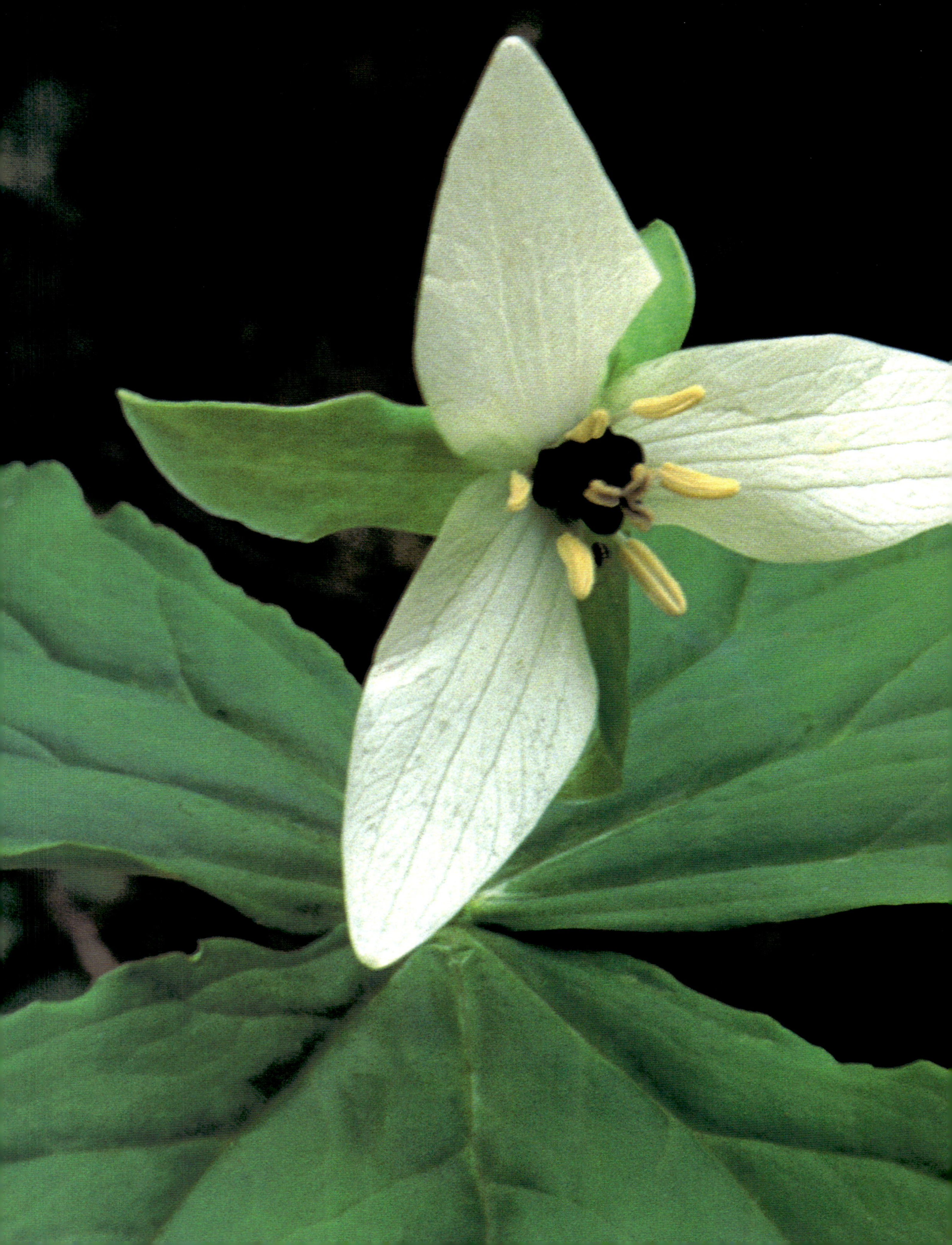

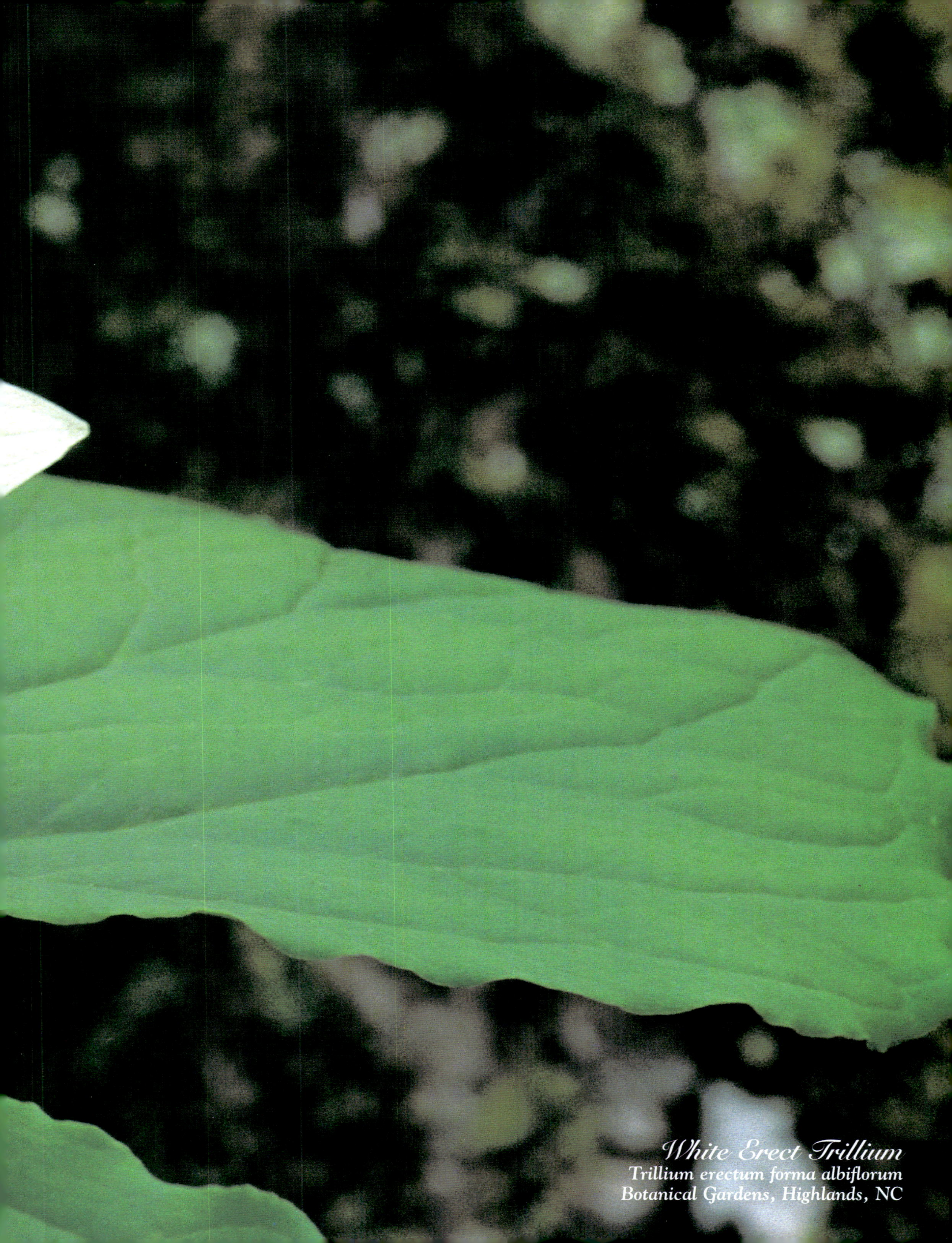

White Erect Trillium
Trillium erectum forma albiflorum
Botanical Gardens, Highlands, NC

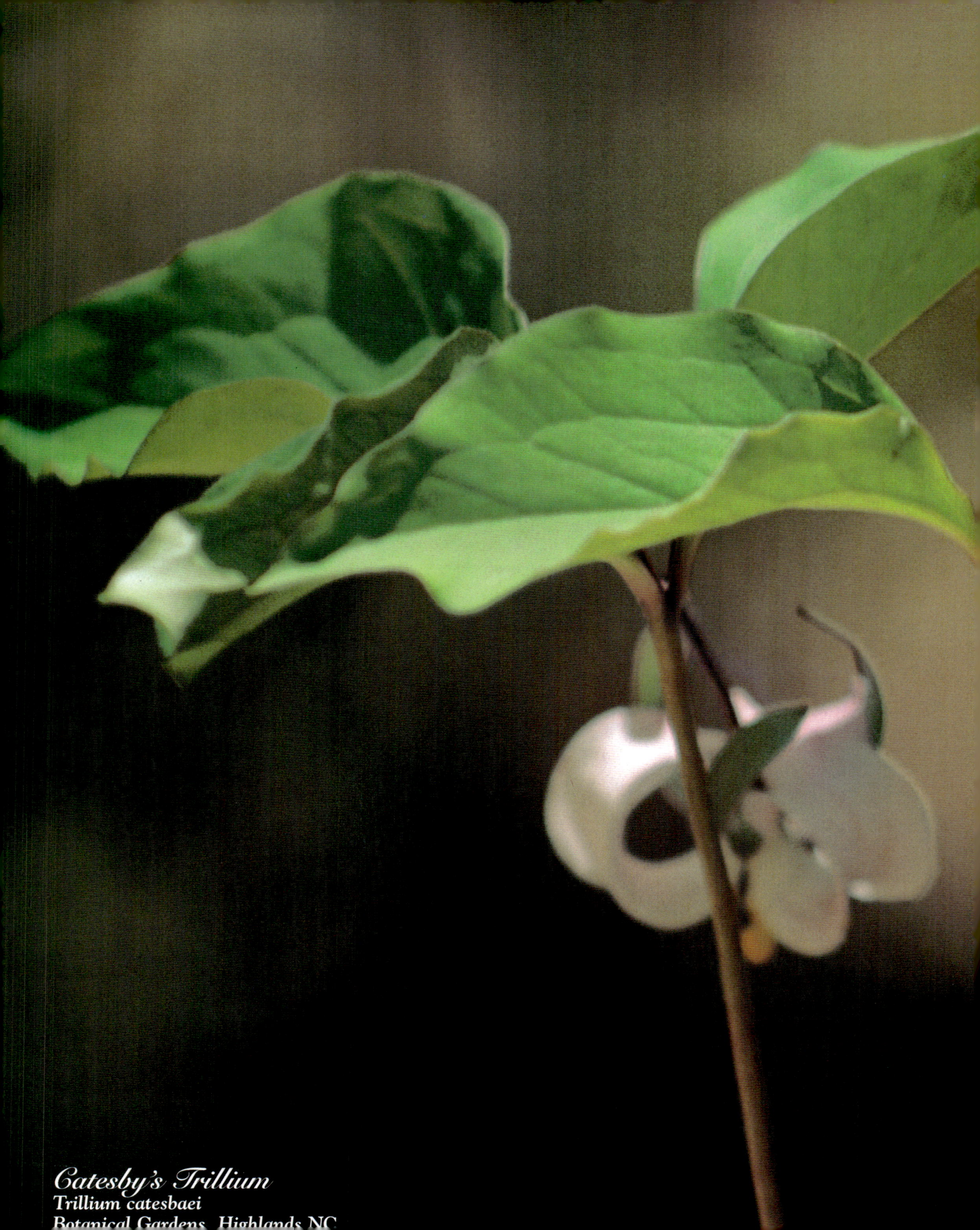

Catesby's Trillium
Trillium catesbaei
Botanical Gardens, Highlands NC

Bouquet of Memories

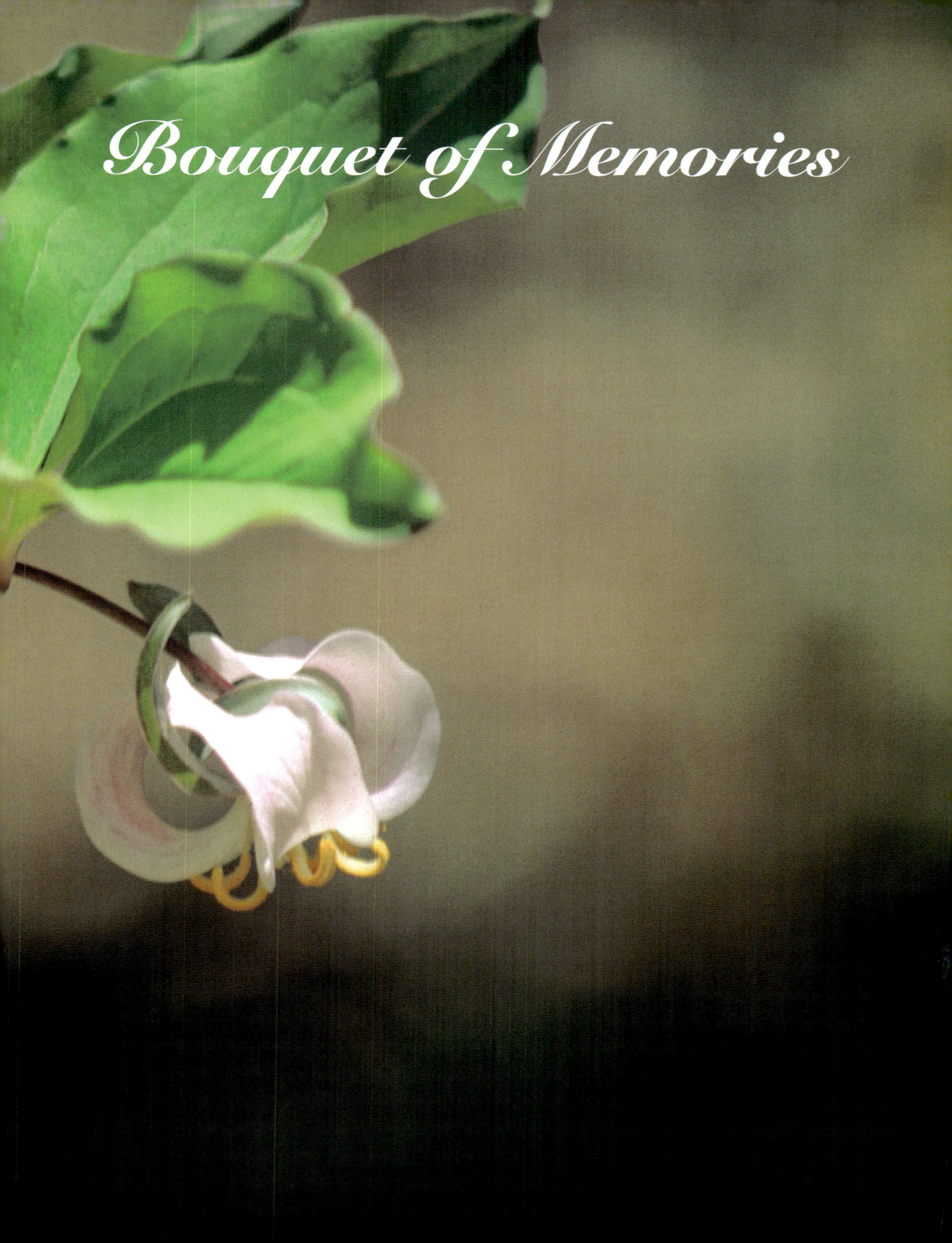

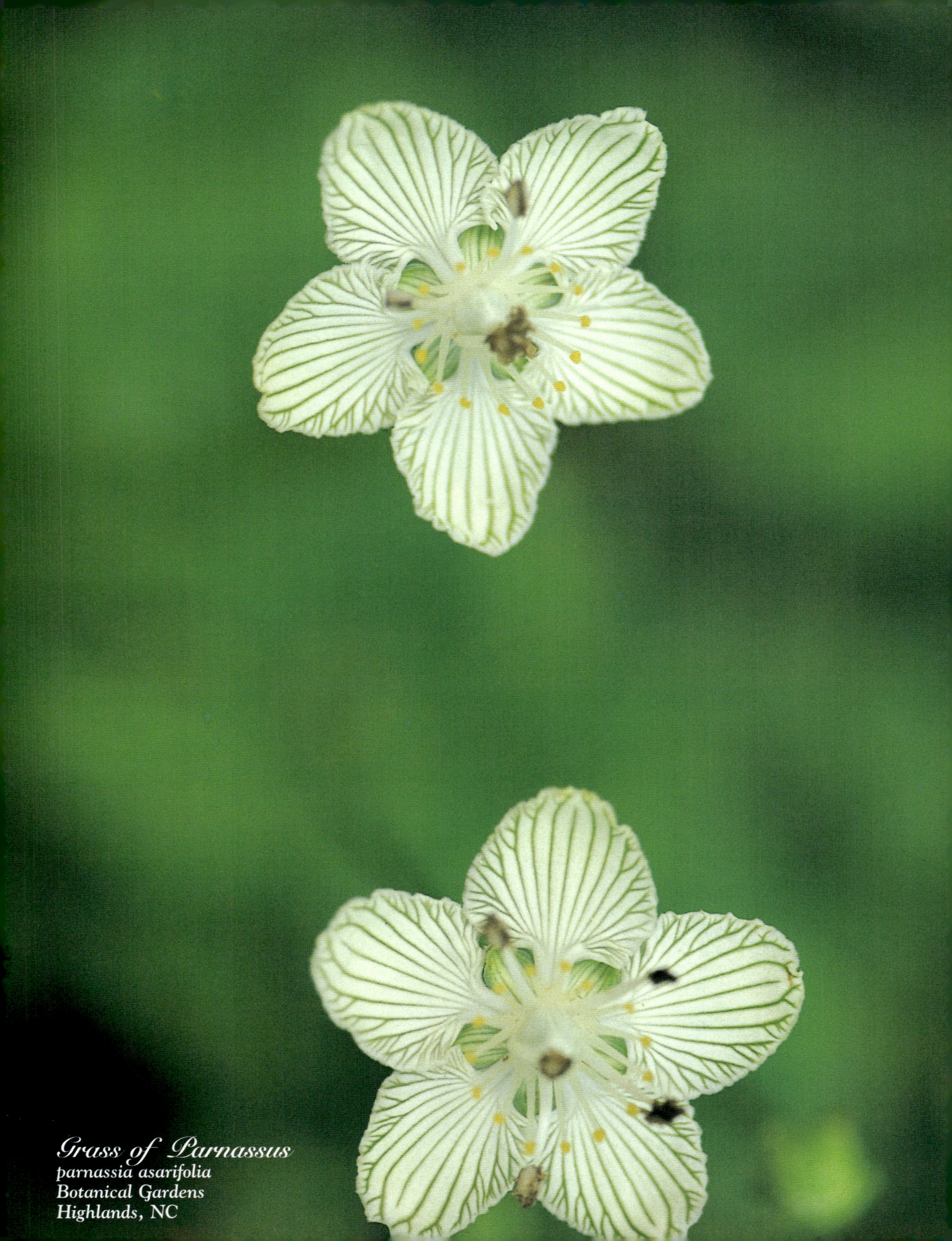

Grass of Parnassus
parnassia asarifolia
Botanical Gardens
Highlands, NC

Bouquet of Memories

"He is happiest who hath power
to gather wisdom from a flower."
Mary Howitt

Among my happiest wildflower memories is a scene of Roy saddling the horses while I walk over to the mountainside to pick wildflowers. It happened several years ago in North Carolina, but I remember it as though it were yesterday. Somehow, it seems to add the finishing touch and complete my bouquet of wildflower memories.

I always kept a tall bucket in the car so I could cut wildflowers to fill the small vases in our mountain cabin. Like a sea of white foam, the sloping hills were overlaid with Queen Anne's Lace. Their small, snowy, multi-layered blossoms were broken only by an occasional wave of yellow and white Daisies. While gathering the round blossoms of beauty from the earth that day, I could see the huge outline of Shortoff Mountain etched courageously against the blue sky. Filled with wonder that such a simple act could produce so much happiness, I clipped the slender green flower stems until the bucket was full. The colorful wildflowers, the cool morning air, the singing birds and a husband nearby made me feel especially thankful that morning.

Leaving the wildflowers at the barn, I climbed onto the squeaky leather saddle. Roy secured the picnic baskets, took his reins, and we started up the National Forest trail. I heard the sounds of the iron horse shoes striking against the rocks and smelled the leather saddle oil and the fresh scent of pine trees. As my body moved in rhythm with the horse's gait, I watched splotches of sunlight fall over spreading ferns and huge Rhododendrons. We climbed higher, not knowing where we were going, but it didn't matter to either one of us. We were on vacation and ready for an adventure. Our trail led along a split rail fence which cupped an old apple orchard and a meadow full of wildflowers.

"Let's stop here and eat our picnic," I said to Roy.

"That's just like you, Janie," he laughed. "You don't even get going good before you're ready to stop and picnic. Let's ride on a little more," he urged, "and we'll come back here later to eat."

We took a new path which led away from the meadow, and rode on, weaving through one trail after another. We passed trees in the ancient forest so big three men couldn't stretch their locked arms around them, and so tall they created an interlaced green umbrella over my head. Roy had always enjoyed trying out new trails. Adventuring was instinctive with him. My ancestors in Pineview, however, always stayed rooted in the same place. But after forty years of marriage, Roy and "Auntie Mame" had finally taught me to appreciate and enjoy trying an occasional new path.

I guess it is not a question though, of whether or not we should follow a different path, but whether or not we have the courage to take a path at all. Paths lead to friends, but they can also lead to problems. Paths can lead to blessings or good fortune, or they can take one in the wrong direction. I seemed to have been moving along all kinds of new paths since reaching the age of fifty...developing interests in inspirational writing, wildlife photography, Roy's new fish camp, our new grandbaby, Janie Lynn, and establishing a Wildflower Ritual. I'd even created a book and become involved in publishing. New paths were all over the place...just like the ones on the mountain there that morning, but new paths are always present at any age if we're willing to look for them.

The metal horse shoes continued to click against the stones as we ambled along the mountain road. Soon, we rode into a clearing carpeted in new green grass, and I began to see fresh cut trees that had fallen along a wide rocky stream. Several clumps of bent orange and yellow Carolina Lilies, once shaded by the fallen trees, were surrounded by fluttering butterflies. The ground was wet in the clearing. We looked down from the horses and thought we saw a huge bear track. Roy got off his horse to measure it and confirm that "Yep! A bear's been here alright."

"Wouldn't it be thrilling to see a bear?" I asked excitedly.

"You might be thrilled," Roy said, "but I'd just as soon we didn't meet a bear up here by ourselves!"

We passed a few fresh-cut tree stumps as we continued to follow the new green grass. Dodging the cut trees scattered across the rocky stream, we stopped dead in our tracks. There before our eyes was not a bear — but BARE, desolate, tree-cut mountains, several mountainsides as bald as a fresh plucked chicken! They looked so naked....acres and acres of clear-cut mountains!

Tears came into my eyes. I felt sad to see such a huge expanse of rain forest cut to the ground. "Look!" I said, shocked at the sight before me, "They've cut every single tree on these mountains. How could they? And...they've planted all this green grass to make us think it's beautiful here!"

"Janie, you know they have to cut some of these trees...,"

"But why?" I asked. "They're in the middle of this glorious rain forest..."

"Sometimes they just have to cut them. They call it 'harvesting' the trees."

"But it looks awful...like a war zone! Someone ought to do something!"

"Janie, you can't fight the Federal Government...," Roy said.

Knowing his passion for trees was not as great as mine, I went on doggedly, "Well, somebody needs to fight them. This is terrible!"

"They've got to take care of the deficit, you know." He laughed.

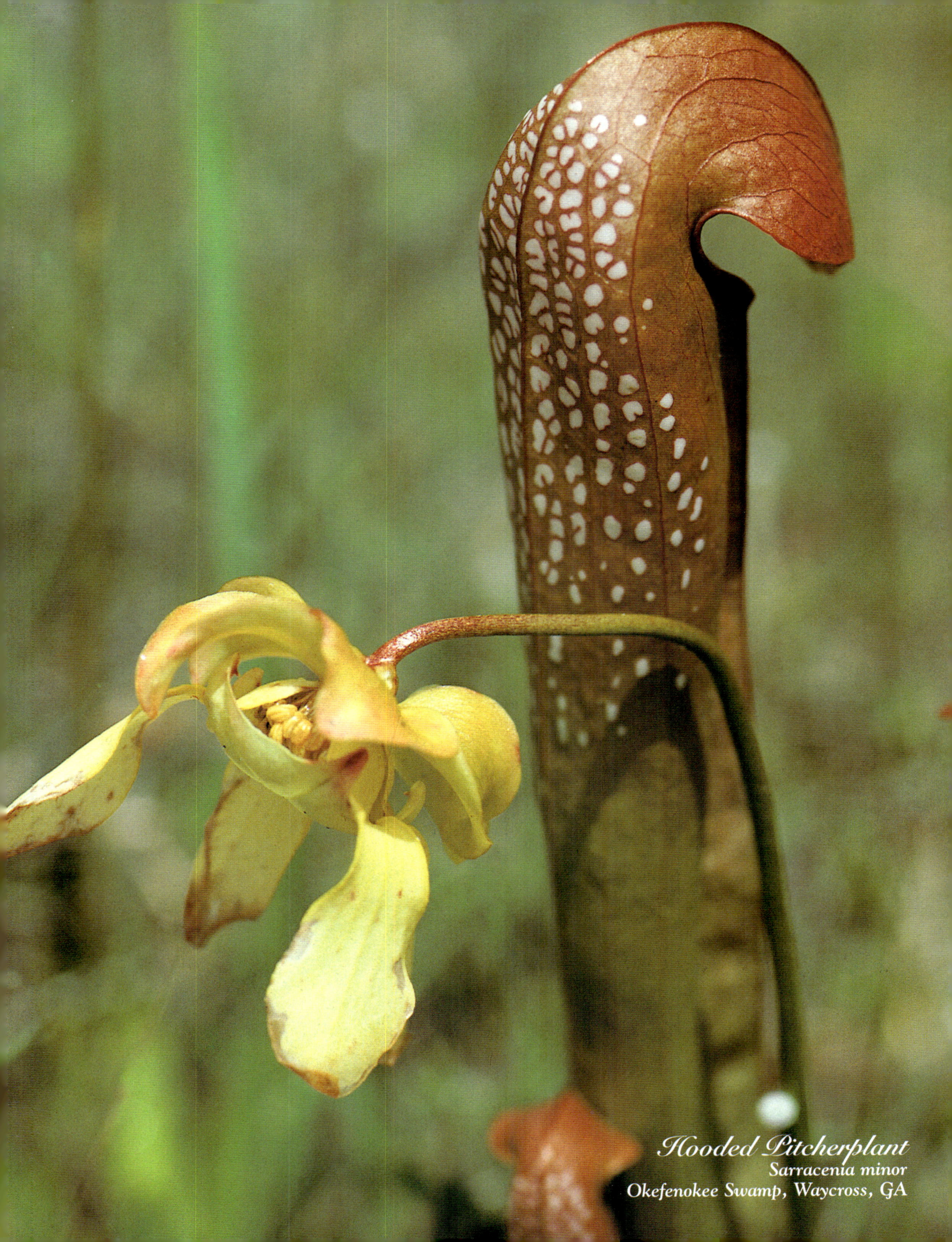

Hooded Pitcherplant
Sarracenia minor
Okefenokee Swamp, Waycross, GA

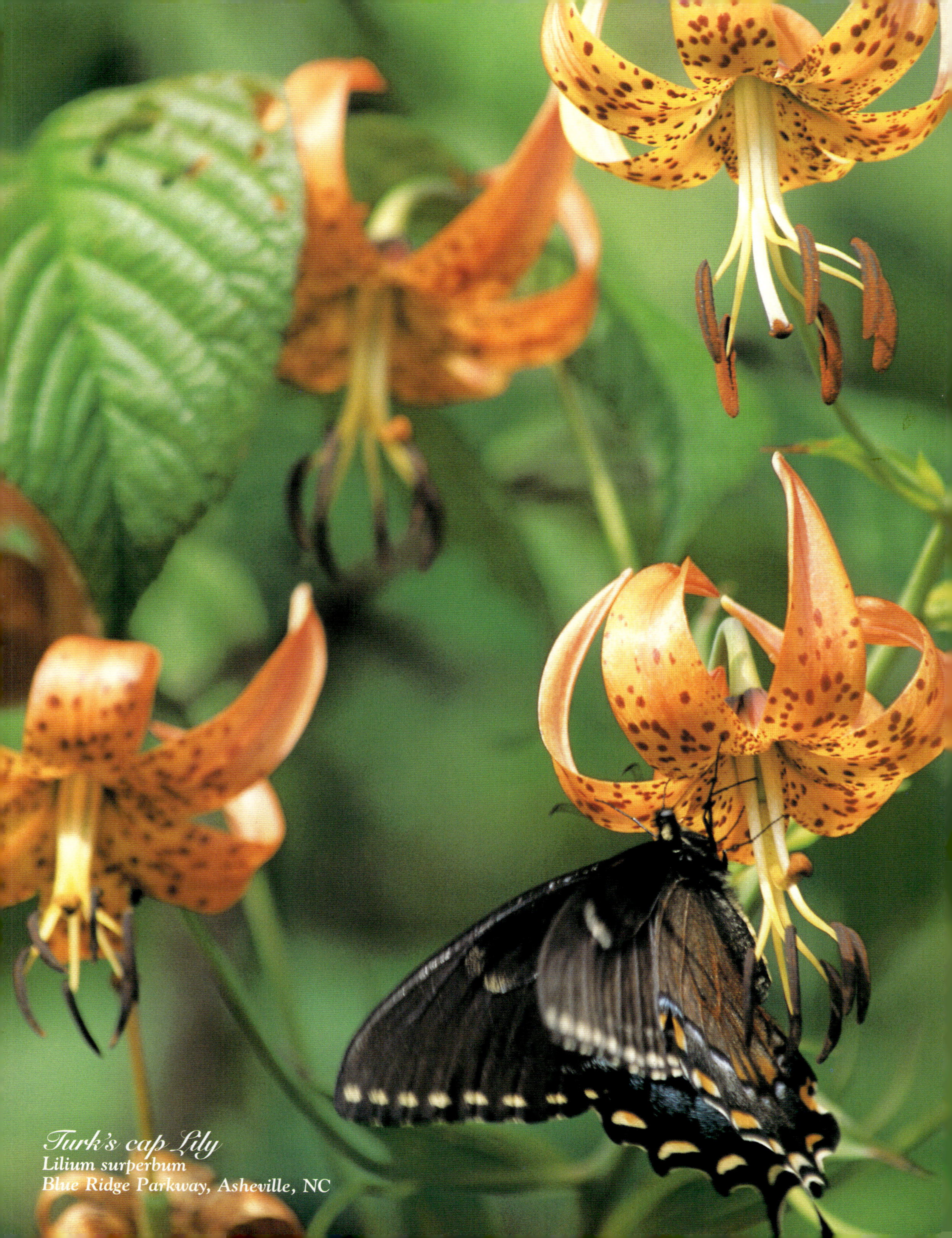

Turk's cap Lily
Lilium surperbum
Blue Ridge Parkway, Asheville, NC

"But our grandparents and parents survived through two world wars and a depression without cutting these beautiful forests. They're our heritage. The National Parks and National Forests are America's greatest assets. Why does our generation have to be so greedy?"

"I wish I had all the answers, but I don't," he said. "Come on, let's get on back to the apple orchard for our picnic."

We started back, but my senses were reeling from the sight of the huge clearing, which stretched as far as I could see. I'd read in the local newspaper about the clear-cutting the government had allowed, but it hadn't prepared me for this shock. Would any of these wonderful old trees be left by the time our new grandbaby Janie Lynne was old enough to ride the mountainside with her husband? How could we complain about cutting the Amazon Rain Forest in Brazil when we were allowing the rain forests to be clear-cut in our country. This temperate rain forest may be small compared to the Amazon, I thought, but ecologically, these rain forests are important too.

I calmed down a little as we rode back into the deep woods where we saw occasional clumps of Carolina Lilies in their natural habitat. They stood tall and straight with butterflies clustering around each lily. In spite of seeing the clear-cut forest, I thought, it had been fun riding along those trails, even when we weren't sure just exactly where we were going.

When we rode back into the meadow picnic area, Roy climbed down and tied both of our horses to one of the apple trees. We spread our lunch there in the open field of wildflowers and sat down enveloped in their light fragrance. There were yellow Black-eyed Susans, Queen Anne's Lace, and Yarrow, all mixed into a field of Pink Clover, so thick you could have made a comfortable bed out of it. There among the low growing apple trees, the split rail fence, the meadow full of wildflowers, I thought I'd never seen a spot so sweet and charming. I placed the moment on one of my imaginary Rosary Beads...a place in the back of my mind where I store a giant collection of happy memories. I'll pull it out again one day, I thought, to touch and finger when I'm too old to get on a horse. Besides we may never stumble on another place like this.

"If I die after this," I told Roy, "I will have known one of the happiest moments my heart would hold." Then I laughingly added, " I can't speak from personal knowledge, of course, but I don't even think Heaven could be any prettier! Growing up in the flatlands of Georgia hadn't prepared me for the beauty of these magnificent mountains!"

The air was warmed by our laughter as Roy and I talked and joked there on the mountain, our voices echoing across the valley. "Hasn't this been fun?" I asked him as we packed up our picnic. "I liked just getting on the trails and seeing where they would lead. I guess that's why there are so many of them. Even though there are many roads which lead to the same place, there are individual ways of getting there."

What kind of road could I take to make a difference in the clear cutting of the forest, I wondered as we mounted our horses again. One way would be to write letters to the governor, congressmen, representatives, and senators. But would that help? Could they do anything? Would they? Where does the answer lie, I wondered. Then I remembered strolling down the Highlands sidewalk one day when I noticed a young family walking close behind me. We passed a hardware store where lumber had been stacked behind a fence.

"Smell that good fresh pine smell," came a feminine voice from the group.

The young boy with them stopped to look through the slat fence at the stacked lumber and said, "I don't like to smell it. It smells like lots of big fresh pine trees have been cut from these pretty mountains." I could hear the disappointment in his voice as he added, "I hate for them to cut the trees!"

I wanted to stop and say to him, "Thank you, Kindred Spirit. Maybe one day when you're a man you'll 'perform the most difficult act of heroism you can perform,' as T. H. White once recommended, and 'go against the dominant thinking of your friends ... of most of the people you see every day.'" But I stopped myself and instead continued on to the drug store to do my errand. I thought possibly the hope of saving our forests lies in our children. Maybe they will take a different path from our generation and revere and care for the living earth. Perhaps one day, they will re-envision America and strive to restore her to her original splendor. They'll realize her treasures are not in money and high-rises, warheads or missiles, but in her jewels in the sand...jewels held dear and precious by our ancestors, our beautiful jewels of the earth...our natural resources. Maybe the seed will even be planted in the minds of some of our grandchildren, like Roy III, John Daniel, or even little Janie Lynne.....and will grow like the scattered seeds of wildflowers until they recognize our forests as one of our nation's most valuable assets.

The forests are not wildflowers, but they set the stage for many wildflowers to grow. Homer D. House, in his book *Wildflowers* wrote on the value of forests to certain wildflowers. Even in 1934 he worried that lumbering would take its toll on certain species of wildflowers when he wrote, "These woodlands of ours are not merely growths of trees. They are the protection, the home and the sustenance of a wonderful variety of wild life. In their shade is the source of waters, the home of wildflowers, countless birds and other forms of wild life."

When I tell my childhood stories, young people today cannot realize that just in my lifetime, I've seen families in America come from a very, very simple lifestyle to the jet age. I've watched families who live by faith and hope and from the breast of the earth. We should and could get back to the land...grab a handful of earth like Scarlett O'Hara and return to our own Tara...our groundedness, our rootedness...to our blessed, sacred earth.

Turning the horses into the pasture, we got down beside the barn and uncinched the saddles from their wet bodies. As we pulled the saddles down from their backs, I was thankful that Roy and I had been on the same path there on the mountain top that day. It didn't take much after all to make me happy...only a few thousand wildflowers, a beautiful mountainside full of giant hemlocks, pines, and deciduous trees, and a husband near me on a clear, cool day.

Through the exploration for *Dancing Petals*, the earth had spoken to me, the wildflowers had whispered, "Come our way," and the memory of Mama's love of wildflowers and Grandma Moore's yard had called out to me....even the Lady-slippers had taught me lessons on focusing my life.

Watching the horses gallop through the field of flowers, as free as the wind, I picked up the bucket of waiting wildflowers I'd left inside the barn. Touching the soft petals, I felt grateful that I had gathered the many wildflower memories, just as I had gathered the bouquet of wildflowers I was holding in my hand. And I knew, too, that just as I'd take the flowers home to arrange inside the cabin, I would also take the gathered bouquet of memories into my heart, mind and soul to become an eternal arrangement there.

Bibliography

INTRODUCTION

1. "I was raised by the song of the murmuring grove and loving I learned among flowers." Fredrick Holderlin (Tr. T. Cole) quoted in Thomas Moore's book, *The Re-Enchantment of Everyday Life* (New York: Harper Collins, 1995, 272.
2. "Heaven lies at your feet as well as over your head." Thoreau

CHAPTER ONE - WILDFLOWER MEMORIES

1. "...The wild geranium holds its dew long in the boulder's shade." William Vaughn Moody, quoted in Helen Steiner Rice's book, *Blossoms of Friendship*, Tarrytown NY: Fleming H. Revell , 1992, 27.
2. "The seeds sown in our lives are in reality, the seeds of our potential. They are sparks of the Divine. They must take root in the earthiness of our lives and grow." Macrinna Wiederkehr, *The Song of the Seed*, New York: Harper Collins, 1995, 8.

CHAPTER TWO - DIVINE SEEDS

1. "Blue! Gentle cousin of the forest-green, married to green in all the sweetest flowers - forget-me-not, - the blue bell, - and that queen of secrecy, the violet." John Keats
2. "Teach us to delight in simple things." Rudyard Kipling

CHAPTER THREE - EARTH'S JEWELS

1. "To see a world in a grain of sand and a heaven in a wildflower; hold infinity in the palm of your hand, and eternity in an hour." William Blake
2. "Afloat and light-hearted, I take to the open road. Healthy, free, the world before me. The long brown path before me leading wherever I choose." Walt Whitman, "Song of the Open Road", *Leaves of Grass and Selected Prose*, New York: Random House.
3. "Live, live, live. Life is a banquet and most poor suckers are starving to death" Broadway musical "Mame." Music & Lyrics by permission from Jerry Herman, diolog by Laurence & Lee. New York, NY.

CHAPTER FOUR - LET THE DANCE BEGIN

1. "For lo, the winter is past, the rain is over and gone. The flowers appear on the earth, the time of singing has come." Song of Solomon 2:11-12, *Revised Standard Version Holy Bible*, Nashville: Thomas Nelson, 1952, 704.
2. "The days when I am happy are the days when I hear music in everything." Anais Nin, *The Diary of Anais Nin*, Orlando: Harcourt Brace Jovanovich, 1980, 237.

CHAPTER FIVE - WILDFLOWER RITUAL

1. "Brief beauty of the Columbine heartens April morn. It bursts its soul in pink and gold flighting moments to adorn." Angela Burns
2. "Choice is the rudder that guides each person's destiny." Alexander Stoddard, *Daring to Be Yourself*, New York: Avon, 1990, 110.
3. "Heaven is under our feet as well as over our heads." Thoreau
4. "... it is often a lack of focus, allowing my energy to run out in dozens of directions, many of them silly tributaries of distraction rather than setting priorities and funneling my energy toward the project at hand. It's true that power can come from the flexibility of doing many things, but sometimes the multiplicity, the moving from one thing to another is overdone and we diffuse our power. There are times it is best to dam up the tributaries and send the energy thundering in just one direction." Sue Monk Kidd, *The Dance of the Dissident Daughter*, San Francisco: Harper Collins, 1996, 208-209.

CHAPTER SIX - HIDDEN BLOOMS

1. "Show me the hidden things. Take me down to the spring of my life, and tell me my nature and my name. Give me freedom to grow so that I may become my true self - the fulfillment of the seed which You planted in me at my making. Out of the deep I cry unto thee, O God. Amen" George Appleton, poem, cover of Annette and Jim Cullifer's Workshop Schedule for Carl Jung Conferences.
2. " Nothing great is created suddenly, anymore than a bunch of grapes or a fig. If you tell me that you desire a fig, I answer you that there must be time. Let it first blossom, then bear fruit, then ripen." Greek writer Epictetus
3. "I learned early in life that I was the only one of me, and I would make the best use of the only me there is." Mickey Rooney
4. "... to be ourselves, we stand on the surest ground." Robert A. Johnson, *Inner Work*, New York: Harper & Row, 1986, 12.

CHAPTER SEVEN - BOUQUET OF MEMORIES

1. "He is happiest who hath power to gather wisdom from a flower." Mary Howitt quoted in Alexander Stoddard's book, *Tea Celebrations*, New York: Avon Books, 1994, 160.
2. "... perform the most difficult act of heroism you can perform and go against the dominant thinking of your friends .. of most of the people you see every day." T. H. White
3. "These woodlands of ours are not merely growths of trees. They are the protection, the home and the sustenance of a wonderful variety of wildlife. In their shade is the source of waters, the home of wildflowers, countless birds and other forms of wild life." Homer D. House, *Wildflowers*, New York: MacMillian, 1974, 7.